I dedicate this book to Eddie's wife Terri, who has brought so much love, care and happiness to his life. Terri, you brought the best out of Eddie, a softer and more accepting side. More importantly, you made him feel complete. The other four special girls in his life were his nieces, who he looked upon as his daughters and he was so proud of each and every one of you. He would light up with love whenever he spoke of you all. Thank you. xx

THE RELUCTANT MEDIUM

Jane Lee

Copyright © 2021 Jane Lee

All rights reserved

Jane Lee has asserted her right to be identified as the author of this Work in accordance with the Copyright, Design and Patents act 1988.

No part of this book may be reproduced, or stored in a retrieval system, or transmitted in any form or by any means, electronic, mechanical, photocopying, recording, or otherwise, without express written permission of the publisher.

ISBN-13: 9798532818903
ISBN-10: 1477123456

Cover design by: Gareth van Rensburg
Library of Congress Control Number: 2018675309
Printed in the United States of America

CONTENTS

Dedication	
Title Page	
Copyright	
The Beginning	1
The Story Begins	4
I'm Lucky to Still Be Here	9
Jumping Forward	14
Hidden Healers	21
Circle Time	25
As One Door Closes Another Opens	34
I Begin to Write	40
Time to Put Down Roots	45
Family Holiday Time	49
As One Chapter Closes Another Opens	58
I Catch Up to See an Old Friend	69
The Gym, A Place of Escapism	74
Time to Take Writing Seriously	81

I Need a Break	87
January 2016 - A Month I Will Never Forget	93
An Interesting Twist	102
An Unexpected Visitor	107
My Heart is Saddened	110
A Date I Will Never Forget	115
Time to Take a Step Forward	123
A New Member of the Family	126
The Calm Before the Storm	131
It's Time for a Rest, Or So I Thought	140
Time to Move on with the Times	143
Time to Work	153
I Didn't See This One Coming	161
Writing a Real Book	168
A Final Farewell	172

THE BEGINNING

Once upon a time, there was a little girl who struggled so hard at night to sleep for fear and dread weighed heavily in her heart. At night, she would see another dimension, a dimension so real, it was tangible. Strange sightings would come and go and this little girl would pray for the morning light.

As the morning light began to appear, this girl's heart would sing a sigh of relief, when the light was bright this tiny might knew she was free to sleep. Finally, a safe place to rest her weary head, for nighttime she would dread. Such a huge burden for one so young. Her innocence and naivety could not, and did not, want to explain the turbulence within her world.

Not only that, but this gentle child would astral travel back home at night. Back home? Yes, to her true spiritual home, a place of safety, unconditional love, acceptance and a true knowing of being where you belong.

Let me set the scene: an old-fashioned wooden house with a welcoming veranda, smoke coming from the chimney, inside lots of familiar people chatting away, three generations, a gentle loving man sat on a rocking chair, very little furniture but such happiness, contentment and love.

I have never felt pure love and bliss like this within. A true belonging and acceptance, I was really loved and treasured. I played outside in the long grass, happily picking wild flowers. I was safe and so loved. All of a sudden, my stomach felt sick, something changed. I felt a buzzing sensation. I saw a fuzzy screen in front of me like a TV that was not connected properly.

The lines were becoming bigger and more jagged. I felt nauseous. I didn't want to go back! Don't make me come back! I felt petrified, my heart raced, the atmosphere felt heavy and dense. Weights were slammed down aggressively on top of my chest.

Darkness! Black, dense, heaviness. I screamed out loud. I was back in the land of the living. This dream, astral travelling that I later learned about, would wake up my poor family every night.

I screamed in fear and despair. Why was I being torn away from my chosen, true home? My parents were exhausted and at one point took me to the doctors as they were so concerned. The doctor reassured my mum it was down to an overactive imagination and I would eventually grow out of it.

I was roughly about three years old and eventually grew out of it, but I never forgot the same dream, night after night and the love, contentment and true acceptance I experienced. I never felt the bliss of electricity and overwhelming happiness and love which I struggled to articulate, until I chose to stop fighting and allowed myself to be the true me.

It has been a long journey, one of bumps and frights in the night but I feel a tremendous amount of honour to work for the spirit world.

THE STORY BEGINS

So, what am I? I'm a medium, a channel for the spirit world. A reluctant medium who spent the first 32 years perfecting the art of not allowing the spirit in. I kept as tight a control over my gifts as possible.

More importantly, I chose not to let anyone know! Did I forget to mention I was brought up in an Irish Catholic family where talking with the other side was not greatly in fashion?

I remember aged 5 being taught in an assembly that it was a sin and evil to communicate with the so-called dead, as they could be dressed up as Satan and be an evil spirit. Nice! So, I chose to sleep at night with one eye open and prayed so hard these people would go away as I wanted to be good, pure and holy like some of the saints we were taught about.

I would know things were going to happen before they occurred and I could feel how others felt. I didn't really enjoy school because all my senses were heightened: the smell of those awful coloured, plastic maths counting bricks, the other children's fear and apprehensions.

When I was 5 years old, we had a school teacher who was a large lady. She always wore trousers, with braces and a shirt, very masculine. I could always smell a faint smell of pipe smoke around her, she felt and smelt poorly. I was frightened of her and I hated going to her class.

One day, she vanished and never returned and was replaced by another teacher. I always wondered what happened to her for there were so many people from the other side surrounding her, as if almost waiting to take her away.

Every Sunday (and I mean every Sunday), we would go to church as a family. It was alright but I would spend the majority of the time watching people's behaviour and the huffs and puffs if anyone dared ask them to move to make way for another to sit down.

Some were so righteous they almost looked down upon others for not dressing appropriately or lacking in education. I remember vividly the gossip about a poor woman who had separated from her husband.

As children do, you're kidding yourselves if you think kids don't hear everything and trust me, if they don't hear, they certainly feel. The disgust and distaste for this poor woman was vile. She would sit in the same place each week with her daughter and you could sense all the daggers of appalled eyes piercing her in the back.

I felt so sorry for her and amused how grown adults could behave so unkindly. For those who don't know, in the Catholic faith when you get married and still today, although more tolerated, it is considered you will remain with each other till death do you part. It didn't matter how awful your life was, that was the condition.

The funny thing was as a child, I remember hearing from all the gossip that the poor lady's husband had left her. However, for some reason, in the congregation's eyes, she was still at fault. For months, this lady would come to church and nobody would talk to her.

Until one day, I suppose she had taken enough and decided to stop coming. But surely as Christians, we were taught to love and forgive one another. None of this behaviour made sense to me especially as one so young. I have to mention, there were some beautiful, kind and selfless people who really were wonderful but it was a mixture.

Every couple of months, usually on a Saturday evening, we were taken to confession. For those who don't know what this is, it's when you go into a tiny box room, kneel down, and a priest, who you can't see, sits in a room next to you ready to hear your sins so he can forgive you with the help of God.

I used to hate this with a passion. Surely, I could tell God myself? I remember I must have been about eleven, my palms were sweaty and my heart was pumping out of my chest. I felt the need to ask the priest why I couldn't tell God my sins by myself and why I had to tell him first.

This was a stupid and silly idea, because in past times you didn't dare and it was considered disrespectful to question the Catholic faith. To even be in a priest's presence was an honour as they were considered so well thought of in society and were hugely respected.

The whole concept of confession didn't make sense to me. I needed to know. I couldn't understand. I had a longing to truly understand why God didn't want to talk to me directly.

The priest sensed my apprehension as soon as I kneeled down to recite my prayers. I remember vividly his gentle, deep voice saying, "Young lady, I sense for some reason you don't want to be here. Why is that?" I was shaking with apprehension and fear because I knew I mustn't question the priest.

Here goes! My parents are literally going to kill me if they find out what I'm about to say. I asked the forbidden question, "Why do I need to tell you my sins when I could tell God myself?" The answer was to trust! Then I was made to recite so many Hail Mary's and Our Fathers, I thought by the time I have finished, my parents would definitely know I have been bad!

As I came out and started my long list of prayers for forgiveness, I prayed so hard the priest wouldn't tell my parents. Luckily for me, he didn't. So, the church for me just didn't feel right. I always felt it was okay as it made my parents happy and proud to see me attend and maybe, that was a good enough reason. Deep inside, I had this strong feeling that I didn't belong and secretly, I didn't want to.

I'M LUCKY TO STILL BE HERE

There are two occasions in my life where I literally shouldn't still be here. I tried hard not to write about one of them, as it still makes me shudder with fear to this day. However, my spirit team deems it best that I share it.

I'll start off with the nice one first. In 1991 I became a qualified Physical Training Instructor in the Royal Air Force and I was posted to RAF Locking, Weston-Super-Mare, a training unit for recruits. This was an awesome place to be sent to as every Thursday night the majority of the station would go out and socialise in the local town.

If you were still standing at the end of the night, you would all congregate in a local night club. We would work so hard during the week and then finally before everyone dispersed to their hometowns, we would literally paint the town red.

I won't lie, we were often so drunk. We were a disgrace. Music would be blaring in the WRAF

(Women's Royal Air Force) block as we all put on our makeup and glad rags to party the night away. I remember all the different perfumes lingering in the corridors and the laughter, excitement and gossiping from all the girls.

I didn't appreciate it at the time, but there was a strong loyalty and protection for one another. We all had something in common and that was, we knew how harsh it was to be in a predominantly man's world. We watched out for one another and always made sure everyone was kept safe.

It was Thursday night again. We started off with our usual pub crawl, followed by dancing the night away in a nightclub. Then it was time for a greasy kebab, chips and finally home. In the town there used to be a pub slap bang in the middle of a one-way system. It used to be nicknamed 'The Coach.'

This was usually the first pub we would start drinking in as it was too dangerous to cross due to the speed of the cars, especially if you were pissed. I don't know why on this occasion we even came this way, as we usually didn't. Oh yes, I remember, someone wanted a burger from a very well known burger chain.

I was feeling worse for wear as I usually did and was walking in front of the group desperate to get back to the Royal Air Force camp. I remember thinking, "Jane, switch on now," as we were crossing the one-way system. The cars sped so fast and stopped for no one. As I was thinking this, I stumbled directly into the road as a car was about to hit me.

I closed my eyes due to fear and then felt a strong firm hand push me back on the path. When I opened my eyes, nobody was there. I remember looking down at my top and physically being able to feel where the car had just skimmed my body. I knew it would have been impossible for me to get out of the way of the car in time.

I turned around to a bunch of girls screaming and crying, huddled up in a ball, consoling one another for they were convinced I had been run over. I walked over and asked what was wrong. I remember my friend Sarah hitting me and shouting, "You stupid idiot! We thought you were dead!" Tears were streaming down her face and then she started hugging me.

We all got a taxi back to the camp but the journey home, usually full of laughter, was silent, sombre and eerie as nobody could work out how I survived.

The second event happened when I was 16 years old. I had lied to my parents and told them I was at a friend's house. The truth was I sneaked off with two so-called friends and we went to a youth club in Reading.

My friends had assured me they would look after

me as I didn't know the area, but they decided to leave without telling me. I was in the middle of Reading and had no clue how to get back to the train station.

I was so naive, innocent and stupid. I really thought these girls were my friends. I remember asking one of the kids what direction the train station was in and then just walked off in that direction. I walked quickly past an area of several large grey commercial wheelie bins. It was dark and I was feeling anxious and on heightened adrenaline.

I heard voices shout out from the bins. I turned my head and saw three white teenage boys, positioning and surrounding me like a pack of wolves. They said I was a dirty whore as they had been watching me come out of the youth club where I had been talking to a black boy. They called me a whore, slag and filthy for talking to a black boy.

I told them I didn't do anything. One of them said to me, "You are filthy and trash. Do you know what happens to trash? The boys then encroached into my space. I wanted to run, scream, fight, do anything but I couldn't. I simply froze! I felt so frightened, I couldn't move. A large booming voice shouted, "Oi, leave her alone!"

A huge tall black guy who I'd never seen before shouted for me to run away and get the hell out of there, then I literally don't know what happened. The power and authority of this voice shook me out of my fear. I ran and didn't stop until I got on the train and was back at one of the girl's houses.

I told them what had happened and was crying, but they weren't bothered. Obviously, I never associated with them again. I often wonder about that guy, who without a shadow of a doubt rescued me from a fate I don't allow myself to even think about. If he hadn't been in the right place at the right time, I would have, at the very least, been beaten and possibly raped.

If I had survived, I probably wouldn't have wanted to. I have no doubt in my mind, this brave man was sent to protect me and is a true earth angel. Thank goodness there are so many kind, good people in the world who have love in their hearts to protect the vulnerable. If by any chance the person who saved me that day is reading this book, I want to say thank you from my heart.

To this day, I still, although very rarely, on occasions have flashbacks of this event. It fills me with such horrendous fear and vulnerability. Having to write this chapter has reduced me to tears and caused unwanted stress but then I have this deep knowing, that for some reason, I am being protected for an important reason. What is it they say? Heaven has a plan for you!

JUMPING FORWARD

Most mediums write about how weird and wonderful their childhoods were and how they saw the spirit world regularly which is fascinating but also a little predictable. I could write a whole book on my childhood but have been told not to by my spirit guides. Maybe one day, who knows?

I'm going to jump to the age of 32. But before that, I'm going to try and convince you, the reader, that I'm actually quite normal. I was brought up in a loving family, one of four kids. As most know, Irish Catholics like big families, the bigger, the better.

As a young girl, I loved playing football and played for a local team. I got selected for the regional squad and I'm proud to say, I was selected for England trials twice. Unfortunately, I was injured on both occasions.

I joined the Royal Air Force as a Physical Training Instructor aged 17 years old. I travelled overseas, taught every aspect of fitness, became a skiing instructor, and specialised in sports injuries and remedial therapy.

She is quite normal, I hear you think! After 14 years, I left the Royal Air Force and became a mother, the best and most important achievement of my life. I was still experiencing lots of spiritual events but amazingly, I managed to keep it a strict secret and under control. Now the fun begins!

Before having my first beautiful child, I had such a severe injury that walking became a struggle. Every footstep was incredibly painful which wasn't great as I was here to help others and keep them fit and healthy.

I had exhausted every avenue but no one could help, so out of desperation, I was told about this lady who had come over from Australia and was an amazing healer.

When you are desperate, let me tell you, you will literally try anything! So I arranged an appointment with this lady who came to my house. Not only was she a healer but she did some form of hypnotherapy and past regression thing. I was not keen on the idea but would like to walk without pain so I thought to myself, "What the hell, let's go for it!"

So the treatment started out nicely. However, when we counted backwards, I had this strange sensation and knowing that I was about to open

Pandora's box. While it was something I really didn't want to open, my desperation to get better was much stronger.

As we talked through the process, I saw in my mind a young girl who told me quite clearly her name was Ruth. I immediately said to the healer, "Did you say Ruth?" She replied, "No." I asked her again. "Are you sure you didn't say Ruth? Somebody had very clearly said Ruth." Pandora's box has been opened!

I took a bath to relax after the healing session. I felt strangely on edge so I closed my eyes and took some deep breaths. My eyes started to flicker out of control, so I opened them quickly. What has that woman done to me?

I tried to close my eyes but it seemed like my eyelids had a mind of their own. I couldn't control the flickering and a bright light sensation in my eyes. I calmed down and told myself this will all pass. I just needed to ignore it.

That night, my eyes flickered out of control each time I tried closing them. I could feel a strong presence surrounding me and my senses were exceptionally heightened to everything. I tried to sleep but couldn't as there was a huge dark shadow presence in my room. I thought if I turned the light on, it would fix the problem. It didn't.

My poor husband had to try and sleep with the

lights on and as soon as I fell into a light sleep, I would scream out of fear as this presence would be looming over me. I tried every past trick in my book at shutting down, like the cloak and bubble technique but to no avail. After several nights of this, I decided to face my fear, on my own.

I went into a zone and asked this presence to show itself to me. I was petrified but I had no choice. What was the choice? I couldn't go on like this and who the hell was I going to talk to? My husband is an amazing, kind and patient man but would he really want to be permanently married to a fruit loop?

So, I went into a zone which seemed like the natural thing to do and said, "Right, show me yourself!" I was bricking it, sorry to be so coarse. To my surprise, a small boy appeared. He had hidden himself in a large cloak to protect himself and his fears. I immediately felt warmth and protection for this little innocent boy.

We communicated through thought, he was basically trapped on the earth plane. It felt like his death was so quick and had shocked him, which meant he didn't go back at the given time. I saw a tunnel of light going up and I really can't articulate what I did but it felt right. It was as though I had done it several times before.

I made the little boy feel safe and assured him he was a big, brave boy and it was his time to go back to his mother who was waiting for him. He seemed so excited and went up this funnel, light thing. I had created so much fear of the unknown but now felt humbled, emotional and honoured to be able to help this little child.

I hoped that was the end of it. Unfortunately, Pandora's box had been opened! Several more children appeared to me and I had to repeat the process many times. Finally, as the intensity started to calm down, I decided to contact the healer again as she seemed open-minded and non-judgemental, perhaps she could help me?

So I went to see the healer and she said those dreaded words, "Sorry my dear, you are a medium. I can't help you." So I thought, "Bloody great! What the hell am I supposed to do now?" This lady has opened me up, now love, you are on your own. Great!

Thankfully, I heard about this shop that sells crystals and offers strange healing courses. So, once again I was desperate and decided to go and ask for help. I was talking so erratically and full of fear that the poor woman behind the counter said she would get someone called Eddie to help me.

Thank goodness, all my problems are going to be taken away and for goodness sake let him close this awful box.

"Alright," in a cockney accent said this bloke in his

late 50s. He was a heavyset, masculine, rough looking man, he had just finished smoking a cigarette. He is the last person you would expect to see in a crystal and spiritual shop. However, I couldn't care less if he had three heads and wings, just make this crazy stuff stop!

We went upstairs to this very relaxing space with wooden beams and lots of crystals and sound drums and things I have never seen before. We sat down and I told him the whole story, eager for him to take it all away. At the end he told me in his deep cockney accent, "Well, there is nothing I can do, you have to control it."

"I beg your pardon? What the F . . . ! Are you for real?" I thought to myself. So Eddie said quite directly and firmly, every time someone from the spirit world comes in, I have to think of him and he will give me strength.

On top of this, it's really important I remain in the material world. To do that, I would need to think of anything in the real world like my plans for tomorrow, shopping lists—anything that can distract my mind from the dead people trying to contact me.

I was gutted. I thought all my problems were going to disappear but no, I had to deal with my worst fears, the spirit world. Eddie was very knowledgeable and knew this was my path. I had to learn how to control my gifts because they were going nowhere. Trust me, I have tried every technique not to be the true me.

I have learnt if you have been chosen, there is no hiding. You just have to decide how you can use your gifts to help others. So I was sent on my way with a very small tool kit and had to face my worst fears. I won't lie, it was incredibly hard and at times I felt anger towards Eddie for not doing more to help. But as the journey unravelled, as always, it made sense.

HIDDEN HEALERS

So off I went, sometimes successful and remaining calm, other times getting overwhelmed with fear, reverting back to the feelings of the five-year-old child who used to cling onto her black and white teddy that magically used to protect her. I took things one day at a time and when I had a good night's sleep, I would feel triumphant.

I was having lots of different treatments for injuries I had acquired over the years, when I met another lightworker who, at the time, hid their gifts from me and still does to society. As a medium, I immediately knew what this person was using wasn't conventional, as it felt completely different when someone is using a healing method.

I approached the person who laughed and assured me it was a technique not commonly used. I knew what he was doing and was told by spirit I was right. I played along with it knowing eventually he would admit the truth.

Let me tell all those readers out there, if someone who specialises in say treatments like massage or osteopathy and has amazing results that other professionals have failed at and are inundated with clients to see them, it's not always down to what they have learnt from the books.

There are amazing and gifted healers who work in professional companies, teachers, the police force, doctors etc., but would never admit to their true self due to being ridiculed, judged or in this day and age, trolled. But don't be ignorant enough to believe these people don't exist, because they do.

In time with me persisting that I knew what treatment I was receiving, he finally felt safe enough to admit the truth. We became friends and eventually, I was introduced to another gifted healer.

I have had the honour of meeting four true healers on my journey. I am referring to people that were born and chosen to heal, not people who have done a couple of courses and think they are experts, which is worrying for this can be dangerous.

These were the first two genuine, gifted healers I had ever met and it was an honour to work with them. They were professional people respected and highly thought of in the community who didn't want to be associated with their gifts due to fear of losing respect and their livelihoods.

I was asked never to reveal their identities and I never will. One of the healers thought they had no spiritual gifts until he had a heart attack, died on the resuscitation table, went through the light and was sent back. His whole life, meaning and thought process was turned upside down. Not only that, his healing gifts were so strong and powerful.

How do I know? I was fortunate enough to receive healing from him and I have never experienced such purity and angelic healing from such a gifted individual. The other person in our little group was phenomenal, one of those people you have to book in advance to get to see.

Another lightworker, humble and hidden out of sight, the way most of us without ego wish to remain. So I finally felt in an okay place, I had found two amazing people and thought this is alright.

I can cope with this even with the new gifts that are becoming stronger, like occasionally being able to see inside people's bodies when healing. I had just started taking my new way of life in my stride.

I was walking through a quaint picturesque village when I bumped into Eddie. We had a little chat and I told him what I had been up to and then he turned around and said, "Right, you can stop all of that. You are ready to sit in my circle." For some strange reason, I didn't even question him because it felt right.

I went to my two gifted healing friends and with a heavy heart told them I was moving on. It was awful because it felt like a betrayal to these two amazing kind people but it had to be done. Perhaps the healing journey was further down the road.

CIRCLE TIME

So I turned up to this circle. I hadn't got a clue what it was but knew I had to be there. The group was predominantly older ladies, who were told exactly where to sit and the chairs were placed in a circle formation.

Now what goes on in a circle, stays in a circle. But I can tell you it generally starts off with a loving prayer and the intention is one of purity and to connect with those in the spirit world. Some religious people will be horrified by this but that is purely down to fear and ignorance.

How do I know this? Oh yes, because I was one of them. Unfortunately, in all walks of life there is good and bad, whether in places of authority like teaching, policing, religious organisations, medical professions etc. Everything in life depends on the hands it is held in, so it's not for anyone to judge unless proven to be corrupt.

This circle was strictly run by Eddie and he was tough. If your evidence was not good enough, you were told to work harder. Eddie was like marmite, you either loved him or hated him. I loved Eddie.

He was a no nonsense guy who said it how it was, harsh at times, but always with a good intention.

His intention was to prove survival after death and we were going to do the same. Everything had to be proven. Eddie gave me the strength to develop my gift. More importantly, he made me feel safe.

I remember in one of our circles, Eddie got frustrated and said in his cockney accent "Right, nobody is forcing you to be here and if you don't want to be a medium, you can stop at any time and walk away."

So at the end of the circle, I asked to have a private word with Eddie and told him I had thought really hard about the situation but had decided I never really wanted to be a medium and didn't want to do it anymore. Eddie quickly replied, "Well, my love, everyone has a choice apart from you. You haven't got a choice so I suggest you just get on with it."

So I asked him why and what I would do in the future and he said I would be a writer, which of course I laughed at. I couldn't be bothered to read a book, let alone write!

Eddie's closed circle was invitation only and was a gentle introduction to circle work as the same lovely ladies would turn up each week. It was full of warmth, kindness and love. The shop the circle was held in was moving location and a new circle was created in another crystal shop but this time in Aylesbury. The circle was also changing to an open circle.

Let me explain to those who don't know what an open circle is. An open circle is where anyone can join and new people come and go each week in the group. Generally, you have a few regulars who build up the energy and then you really won't know who will attend.

It's a great place for keen and up and coming mediums to practise their connection as you know nothing about the people who will attend. Therefore you have to connect with spirit to find information only the person receiving the message could possibly know.

This is the difference between the waffling medium and a good medium. Eddie took no prisoners. If you couldn't come up with evidence, you were told to go back and work harder. I loved Eddie for his no nonsense, tough teaching approach. It often upset so-called experienced mediums and they didn't last long in his group.

Eddie passionately wanted the best evidence and connection to the spirit world. Perhaps one day it would be scientifically proven life really does continue after the physical body dies.

So now I'm in an open circle, the fun really begins. Unfortunately, not every person who attends should be there or has such a longing for all their problems to be resolved. With such a variety of energy, it was harder to work through all the different vibrations and baggage people bring with them.

I hear an outcry from all the open circles in spiritualist churches. In a spiritual church, you tend to get people who want to be there and have more of an understanding. Not always, but generally. In this little shop in the middle of Aylesbury town centre we got such an extreme, diverse mixture of people who let me assure you, wouldn't step foot in a church.

It was such a steep learning curve and one I will always be thankful for, as the experience I gained was fast, tough and quick. This was where my foundations were laid.

I remember an Italian man in his 60s used to turn up every week. He carried so much anger and aggression in his heart, it used to frighten a few of the group. Yes at times, even myself. Each week, he would turn up and each week, we would look at Eddie with pleading eyes, as if to ask, "When are you going to get rid of him?"

I had the privilege of connecting for him. His life was one of great sadness. As a child, he had so little, a bed and on the wall a little wooden crucifix. He had been brought up as a strict Catholic and was regularly beaten by his father. The fear he felt was tangible. He loved his mother but felt betrayed as she never tried to protect him, but also he knew she couldn't.

His beautiful, loving mother came through and described and showed me his childhood and all the memory links including his one treasured possession which was a bible. His mother asked for forgiveness and gave him a heartfelt message which only he understood.

Within that precious time you could literally see this man transform and release all his anger. He became really emotional.

We had the honour of witnessing healing in front of our eyes and the power of the spirit world. I also need to mention that when you work for spirit and relay the message to the loved one, you get the feeling and sensation of all the love from the spirit person to the recipient.

It literally fills your whole body with an explosion of euphoria physically and mentally. Imagine true love running through your veins! The medium is literally the channel of communication in the middle of two loved ones (though not always the case).

After that session, this less angry man would throw his arms around me every week and treat me as though I was some sort of holy saint, which was a little embarrassing. But it came from a good place. I'm sure you might have gathered, I'm definitely not a saint!

A few weeks later, Eddie was really kind and gentle to this man and asked him to leave the group because it wasn't the time for him to be developing as a medium. I asked Eddie why it took him so long to remove this man as it was obvious to the group he wasn't going to be a medium and at times he was quite aggressive.

Eddie replied we all needed to learn the sensation of hurt, pain and anger. So what if it made everyone feel uncomfortable, it wasn't about our needs, it was about this man not being turned away and given an environment to process and heal. The easy option would have been to have turned our backs on this gentleman due to fear.

Eddie always pushed the boundaries and was reassured by the spirit world the outcome was safe. So weekly, for a few years, I would sit religiously every week working hard to perfect the connection from the spirit world to the recipient. I loved working.

It was the only thing I found natural, fulfilling and truly inspiring. The only thing that hindered my progress was me, due to that dreaded word fear. I would make connection after connection for others and prove the survival of their loved ones but just couldn't believe in myself.

The fear I felt as a child, being scared of the visitors at night, coupled with taught religious beliefs, has held me back. Circles are amazing developing environments for mediums, a safe place to develop but you must always ensure the leader is experienced, has full control and the ability to protect the group.

Circles are not to be played at, it is very real. I believe if you haven't got a calling or a desire to use your gifts to help mankind in a positive way, don't bother. Life is complicated enough without adding more problems (just my opinion).

So the occurrence I am going to mention once again will upset those who believe everything is airy fairy and there isn't any negativity within a circle, as long as you put out the right intention and pray to an Archangel. I hope those who disagree are those who have never had a negative experience, as I wouldn't want you or any other to have this experience.

I am really thankful as it has taught me that the higher the vibration you work in, the more protection you will receive. As I said before, an open circle can invite all sorts of wonderful, magical and very interesting energies.

So once again, it was circle night. We sat down, sent out our positive intentions and asked for protection for all the circle members. I remember vividly, that night felt odd, strange and dense. As the circle continued, we gave messages which were received with gratitude.

I forgot to mention Eddie made me sit to the right of him which he hadn't done before. He told me in his rough cockney accent, "Jane, I want you to sit next to me tonight. I need to keep an eye on you." You never questioned Eddie, not unless you were stupid. So I got up and sat next to him.

As the circle progressed, I noticed peripheral things flying around the room, like see through veil material. I am struggling to articulate as I can't find the right words. Basically, there were things flying occasionally out of nowhere around the room. Every time I tried to look at them, they would vanish so it was only out of the corner of my eye that I could see them.

Normally, I would see inside my mind but tonight it was everywhere. This was how I would see it as a child but learnt to shut it down. It was all coming back tonight. Eddie didn't say a word but made me hold his hand, which trust me, I was more than happy to do. I then felt something so dark, evil and harrowing. I froze.

This dark evil presence was encroaching my space, I shuddered and felt sick. Then I felt anger. I shouted in my mind, "BACK OFF!" I literally and naturally forced energy from myself pushing this dark thing, an entity, I really don't know what, away from me with enormous force and shouted in my mind, "NO!" It disappeared.

For that moment, I took full control and learnt nothing can harm you. But you need to be strong and in complete control. I told Eddie what had happened and he said, "So you controlled it, how did that make you feel? You are always in control Jane, move on."

"What move on? Are you for real? A bloody evil thing just came up to me and you want me to move on?" Eddie was right. I had learnt who was in charge. There is no place for fear because fear fuels lower energy which is negative. The higher frequency and more positive energy you surround yourself with, the more protected you are.

So basically in life, whenever you feel low, try to send positive thoughts out or at least dig deep and look at all the wonderful things in your life, even if it's the clean air you breathe. Gosh, where did that come from? That was preachy!

AS ONE DOOR CLOSES ANOTHER OPENS

I'm sad to say Eddie's health started to deteriorate and he found the long journey from Portsmouth to Aylesbury too much. This selfless person would travel miles every week, paid just enough to cover his petrol money to help develop mediums.

He worked as a medium in the churches. I heard he upset a few presidents on the way, but that was just Eddie. Eddie was at times too truthful, harsh and a task master but if you knew him properly and dug a little deeper, he really was a beautiful soul. He never judged others and worked purely for spirit for no personal gain.

I kept in contact with Eddie throughout my journey as he was the only person I felt safe and trusted. I would ring him regularly with panic stricken telephone calls explaining what I would see and experience. Trust me, there was no one else in the world I would share the weird and often frightening occurrences with.

They were only frightening because I didn't understand what they meant, which was always explained bluntly and straight to the point. There was no flowering up or gentle explanation, it was explained in truth and honesty. Sometimes, I would struggle to come to terms with the truth, but Eddie would always reassure me and tell me to pull myself together.

Eddie made me feel so loved, protected and strangely strong. I could and would overcome anything with him by my side. At night, I would get regular visitors and be shown flying objects of light which I would really struggle to articulate without sounding ridiculous. So let's just say things the average person doesn't always see.

Then as I progressed. I would start seeing orbs on the ceiling whilst watching TV and an occasional fly or a spider running across the floor which I knew wasn't really there. I would also see people walking by out of the corner of my eye.

Again, they weren't really there. This information was for Eddie's ears only. I wondered at what point he would tell me to seek medical help because he wouldn't break the news gently to me, that was for sure. So I would ring him with apprehension, worry and fear in my voice and explain the orbs, insects and people.

Eddie would sigh, always take a deep breath and then in his deep cockney voice say, "It's nothing to worry about love. You'll get used to it. It's just another dimension you're seeing and the orbs are just spirits. It will come and go. Try and enjoy it and hold it for as long as possible. It's really quite interesting, nothing to worry about, Jane."

Great, I'm now seeing invisible people during the day and other dimensions. What a bargain, lucky me! Once I got over the shock, understanding and amusement of what I was being told, I always felt reassured and accepting for Eddie might have been many things but he always spoke the truth.

I remember thinking, "What the hell am I supposed to do now? I've lost an amazing teacher but more importantly, a person I respected and trusted." These two things are so important when finding a teacher.

You don't always have to like them but you must have respect and trust. I fortunately kept in touch with one other member of the circle, a lovely and very talented medium, Becky.

Becky would search for the next best teacher and soon came along a very well known and respected medium, Heather. Heather dedicated her time to studying mediumship, what aspects of the brain we would work and all the science behind it.

She was an instructor at a well known College

of Spiritualism and psychic sciences, has read for well-known celebrities and even helped the police solve a crime the majority of you would have heard of.

Becky started in Heather's circle and was really impressed, so I asked if I could be considered to join. Much to my delight, Heather agreed. This circle was held in Heather's living room, with at the time, a total of five people.

Heather had such a scientific approach to teaching. She wouldn't just accept it as spirit but needed to know how the physiology of the brain worked when we were connecting and what aspects we were working with.

Heather was refreshing because she wanted to prove to the world the science behind mediumship, so hopefully, one day, it would be scientifically proven. Please don't expect me to tell you how the science of the brain works when we are connecting to spirit. It's all fascinating but above my intellect.

Heather was a strict, kind lady who worked tirelessly to find the best methods to get the most accurate evidence out of the mediums. She was completely selfless, constantly using and sharing different teaching methods to work us hard.

She would teach us to go into the home of the connected spirit and describe in detail what it looked like in each room, the pictures on the walls, the colour of the carpet, their possessions, the smells, the feelings, how it felt.

If the loved one had a garden, describe it, memory links. Heather pushed for more and more evidence. She was a task master. She passionately wanted a high standard of medium to go out into the world with the right intention. Not those that could simply connect but didn't have enough proof to back it up.

I spent roughly 18 months in Heather's circle and gained even more knowledge in such a short period of time. She had shared her wealth of knowledge and given us all a wonderful spiritual toolbox to take on our next journey. I'm eternally grateful to have had the opportunity to sit in a circle with one of the most gifted mediums that exist today.

Heather had decided to move to a different area. So once again, the circle came to an end. It's really quite sad when you leave a circle because the trust and friendships blossom quickly and there are no secrets to be hidden. The spirit world tends to inform you especially if someone needs to process past or present hidden issues, nothing is off limits.

In closed circles which Heather's was, you have to commit to attending every week for you have made a time and date for the spirit world and unless literally you physically can't get there, you will attend.

This time set aside has to be more important than the material world so the whole group can move forward. The older, more experienced teachers insist on this. I believe it is the correct way for you shouldn't have people playing at this.

It needs to be taken seriously and you need to ask yourself why you want to do this. Mediumship isn't for entertainment, it's a gift to help heal others, hopefully reduce the intensity of their grief and to start healing, knowing their loved one is safe and happy. I genuinely can't think of a more important responsibility.

This is also the reason why mediums need to spend time perfecting their gifts, not get overexcited and set out too early. Otherwise we can cause more damage than good. It's all about the client's needs, not the mediums. And this takes time to mature (just my opinion!).

I BEGIN TO WRITE

So I was at home breastfeeding a newborn, potty training a two-year-old, why, I can't wait until the child turns three. Oh yes, my nanny friends tell me this is a must. I forgot to mention I'm trying to get my five-year-old out the door to school before my youngest creates a breast feeding runny poo out of the sides of her baby grow.

Life is hectic, but I love it! And I am so grateful to be a mum as we really weren't even sure I was going to be. Miracles do happen, so never give up!

This was the time in my life that I started feeling overpowering urges to write. I would be sitting having a quiet moment which was such a rarity, usually when the kids were either at school, pre-school or asleep.

I would find myself erratically searching for pen and paper. I would sit down and write, had no idea what I would write, I just had to write. When I read the words back, I knew they weren't from me because they were beautiful and had deep meanings. As much as I would like to pretend to be an inspirational writer, I can't as I would be lying.

I struggled passing my GCSE English but we won't tell the kids that one. I would read the writings to my mum over the phone and she would say, "Well, you haven't written that. That's really clever Jane." How rude, but completely true!

I would get really excited about the writings I was channelling from the spirit world. I would find them fascinating as I had no idea what I would receive. I would share them with my mum as I had no one else to talk to. I hadn't even told my closest friends that I was a medium because I had such a strong fear of being judged. Quite sad really but that's how I felt at the time.

I didn't want to be considered bad, a witch or working with dark energies as I knew that I was working with something so beautiful, pure, light and loving. At the same time, I felt it was impossible to convince others, especially those with strong religious backgrounds.

There is often so much fear of the unknown as I myself have experienced. The last thing I wanted was to be labelled and more important considered some sort of evil, dark person. Oh gosh, my Catholic schooling taught me better than I thought at the time!

I would be watching TV and suddenly say to my husband, "I'll be back in a moment." He knew I would be upstairs in the bedroom as at the time this was the only quiet place. I wrote and wrote until I was told to stop. I had books and books of writings. I eventually moved from pen and paper to computer which became second nature.

As the kids became older and more settled, I would programme in time slots to write with my spirit team which was an honour as it became such a pure channel. It would lift me up both physiologically and mentally. I would feel on such a high after writing. It became my saviour from the material world and all the hardships we all encounter.

I asked my guide why I was writing and they said I would go on to publish a book and eventually my work would help others. I was a bit sceptical but I was intrigued to see if this would materialise as I hadn't any desire to write a book.

I even thought it would be funny if it came true. I mustn't forget to mention whilst all this writing was going on, I noticed an increase in strange things happening especially at night.

I was starting to become less fearful of visitors at night from the spiritual world. I think this was down to exhaustion as I was looking after three young kids. Apparently, if you are a medium, you are like a beacon of light to the other side so it would make sense some of them will want to have a closer look.

Eddie taught me I needed to take control, which

most of the time worked, but occasionally, I would get a fright. One night, fast asleep, I woke up to a huge dark presence best described as a thick dense shadow leering over the top of me. It felt awful, fearful and I couldn't catch my breath.

It was like I was under water, drowning in fear. I've had lots of different experiences but the fear was tangible. Of course I dealt with the situation very maturely, screamed and woke my husband up. My poor husband, he really is a martyr. So the next day, I felt quite perturbed by the situation so I rang my good friend Eddie up.

I would ring Eddie when strange occurrences would happen and if he didn't know he would always find out which was brilliant. As the saying goes, "Knowledge dispels fear" although as I have found out throughout my journey, not always. But I would rather understand than bury my head in the sand.

I explained the situation in great detail to Eddie making sure I didn't leave out any details. He replied in his no nonsense, straight to the point rough cockney accent, "Well my love, it just means something awful or someone is going to die in the next three, days, weeks or years. It's just a premonition they are usually negative, from my experience, you don't usually get good ones."

"Oh well, that's alright then. Something to look

forward to!" I thought. It was times like this I would have liked Eddie to have broken the news a bit more gently but I was thankful for his frank help and support. Sad to say, within exactly three weeks a huge cruise ship crashed making the news and several people lost their lives.

I was really upset and this weighed heavy on my heart for there was nothing I could have done to have prevented this event. It made me feel angry. Why show a person such a catastrophe if they can't help? This is one of the downsides of being a medium, knowing an outcome but literally not being able to do anything about it.

The dark presence made sense, I felt I was drowning, couldn't breathe and the fear was so strong it was thick and in the air. Thank goodness to date this has only happened three times throughout my life. Eddie, unfortunately, is right. It usually results in a sad ending.

TIME TO PUT DOWN ROOTS

Being married to a military man, it was time once again to go on our travels. But this time, we decided to put down some roots. So, we finally have roots, a strange concept as we haven't been settled in civilian street for over 18 years. I've left everything I've known and now need to fit in again. You get used to not fitting in, then fitting in and then being 'Billy no mates' again.

After a period of time, my first priority was to concentrate on the kids, making sure they have the best schools, pre-schools and toddler play groups, I felt overwhelmed to find another spiritual circle. There is a Spiritualist church down the road but I'm not overly keen on going anywhere near a church environment. I literally didn't know anyone, it was tough, but I knew I had to start somewhere.

The dreaded day came. I sat in a church environment (which I would rather not be in) once again, but this time in a circle. I was pleasantly surprised to be welcomed by lots of like-minded, lovely middle-aged and older ladies. It was calm, all very lovely and unthreatening. A complete contrast from Eddie's circle where literally you didn't know what colourful character would walk through the door.

I religiously attended this circle every Monday evening for several months before I was invited to join a closed circle. This was an honour for only those who are considered ready or have proven they have a good connection or potential to work with spirit got invited to a closed circle, especially in a church environment.

I met my new teacher. I expected a softly spoken, gentle older lady who is going to nurture all our strengths and improve our weaknesses. Wrong! Dorothy, an average sized, older lady with peppered coloured wavy hair and strong piercing eyes greeted us.

You know as soon as you meet Dorothy she means business. Time with spirit is her life and you will conform, work hard and listen. No messing around in this circle.

I was excited because I came from a military background. I was not there to play either and wanted to learn as much as I possibly could. Dorothy would not be everyone's cup of tea but once again, she was perfect for me.

I have to mention something else about Dorothy, which not everyone will know and that's as you get closer to her and she allows you to see beneath her layers, she was one of the most selfless, kind women with a huge heart who just prefers her spirit guide and animals to humans.

She has dedicated her whole life working with spirit and helping develop other mediums to produce a safe environment for them to work in. Dorothy is an exceptionally talented and gifted medium, who I deeply respect. Each week, we would meet up, only a small group of six. No 'airy fairy' nonsense straight to work.

Dorothy's circles are led by her spirit guide and are diverse, clever, creative and challenging. She would get us to stand on the podium at the top of the church as though we are working mediums and prove the survival of loved ones. Again and again, she worked us by pushing our boundaries and wanting more and more evidence.

We were challenged with connecting and giving speeches with no preparation on words picked by Dorothy. Trust me if it's not good enough you are told, no messing. The beauty of a closed circle is, you become connected very quickly as you learn each other's vulnerabilities and stories you have usually hidden away for good reasons.

You see each other's true strengths and weaknesses which as humans we have learnt not to expose in the material world. You will always feel more drawn to some circle members than others but you will develop an appreciation for everyone. Everyone has a story, a happy or sad childhood, a frightening and traumatic event or a deep sadness buried within.

If the spirit world wants you to process this, it will be revealed and trust me, there were some heartfelt stories shared. Another thing to mention is the strong trust within the group. What went on in the group, stayed in the group and was not to be spoken of.

Hence, I will not reveal information for your entertainment although it would blow your minds and make this book a lot more interesting. One thing I can share which might amuse you is literally when we needed confirmation, the church lights would flicker on and off to confirm the information we received was true, a bit creepy but true.

FAMILY HOLIDAY TIME

The one thing I am really not into is paranormal activity. I don't really like the dark, can't watch horror movies, but I'm getting more happy and comfortable speaking to spirit people. Work that one out, I can't!

So I've frequently sent out thoughts saying, "I'm more than happy to work for the spirit world but you must under no condition start moving objects around my house or do any of that crazy stuff as I literally can't think of anything worse."

I don't need them to show me any of that paranormal nonsense because I've made enough connections and proven it time and time again, all of this is very real. So let me tell you an interesting story. We were all so excited we worked hard, saved our money and managed to get a holiday to, wait for it, Tenerife!

A family of five with three kids under seven, so it's not going to be a relaxing holiday but it's so wonderful to be getting away. We arrived to be told our apartment has been changed but thought nothing of it. We walked in, it felt strange and looked a bit dirty. We called reception and two cleaners arrived to quickly give it a once over.

The cleaners seemed on edge and couldn't get out of the building quick enough. I sensed something odd and the vibration in the apartment felt eerie. I didn't mention anything to my husband as I don't want that look of "Here she goes again." The apartment is a duplex but I'm not happy for any of the kids to sleep downstairs without me.

Tony humours me, so we all sleep upstairs, with all three of the kids crammed into one room with a sun lounger and a blow up lilo on top of it. Thank goodness, the youngest is only light. The kids think it is all an adventure and are excited to be together, they just saw it as a sleepover.

The apartment felt strange. I can't sleep at night and I keep getting what is best described as a bright light shining in my eyes. I decided not to mention anything to Tony so as not to spoil the holiday. Tony after a few nights says, "I don't know why but I just can't sleep." So I also mention the lack of sleep.

The following night the lights in the bathroom kept switching on and off and loud noises occurred from the above extractor fan which is a little unsettling. Tony, with an engineering background, goes to sort out the problem. Surprise! No problem found. We tried to go back to sleep, but I found myself repeatedly checking in on the kids as I felt unsettled and the lights continued to randomly flicker.

Strange noises also kept coming from the bathroom, but eventually everything settled down. I felt very uneasy but pretended to go along with the electrical problem. We got an electrician out who assured us there was no problem but can't explain why this has happened. He looked at us as though we were foreign idiots, Tony is one hundred percent convinced all of this is electrical.

The following night, we felt content, relaxed and really looking forward to a good night's sleep. We have had a full day, entertaining the kids in the pool, making sand castles, mud pie cakes on the beach and shell hunting. We are definitely going to sleep tonight.

In fact, I think we will pass out after a couple of glasses of wine, we were shattered. Lying in bed, I had a strange feeling of a presence in the room and a bright light appeared in my already closed eyes. I decided not to mention anything and hoped it would disappear. But I was wrong.

Here we go again, the lights start to flicker in the main bathroom, the extractor fan turns itself on and the electrical box starts to flash numbers. Before we had time to check what's going on, the whole apartment went pitch black. Then the lights switch on again, and the extractor fan turns itself on full blast.

Tony goes in to sort out the electrics, now it doesn't matter what he does, all the gadgets are out of control. Eventually it settles down, I'm feeling on heightened edge because the presence in this building is so strong. I need to hold my nerve and not fuel this situation with my fear.

We finally got back to bed, let's try again. Oh my gosh! Someone is downstairs. We can hear the stools in the kitchen being moved and scraping across the tiled floor. Crashing and banging downstairs, we leapt out of bed. "Please Tony, don't go downstairs, you could get killed!" I begged him not to go downstairs.

I was sent to protect the children. Our adrenaline and fear were heightened to the point of literally fight or flight. We are going to fight! Tony grabbed a pair of sharp scissors from the bathroom and headed downstairs. I was ready to kill whoever comes upstairs to protect my children. The military training took over and we were ready to die in battle. (I have never been so scared in all my life!)

Trust me, I have jumped out of planes, skied down black runs, canoed in rough waters but nothing has scared and horrified me like this. Tony went downstairs, nothing! He turned on the lights, nothing! He searched under the beds, cupboards, balcony, nothing! It's eerily quiet as though no one has been in, but the stools have been physically moved across the room.

Something you would definitely notice as we decided not to use the breakfast bar and stools to prevent any of the kids hurting themselves. I decided to go downstairs to double-check as there is no way I'm going back to bed without checking the whole apartment. Ladies, as you know we are better at finding things, nothing!

We lay in bed, hearts still racing trying to work out what the hell just happened. Somebody was downstairs. We both heard it, the stools were scraping across the cold tiled kitchen floor. Not to forget the lights, flickering off and on and the extractor fan turning on by itself.

You could feel the presence of people in the apartment, this did happen. If I had been on my own, nobody would believe this story but Tony witnessed it all. Trust me, he doesn't believe as he calls it, all this spiritual bollocks!

The next day, I felt compelled to find out if there was anything spiritual going on in the apartment. While I've had the training and an inner knowing of how to deal with the situation, I don't feel in any way the desire or bravery to do this on my own.

I felt angry, how dare any harm come anywhere near my children! That protective streak was enough for me to face whatever it is that was behaving in a threatening way.

Tony went out for a run. I put a children's DVD on for the kids and told them they must not come anywhere near me unless it's an emergency. I confidently told Tony I'm going to deal with the situation and when he gets back it will all be sorted. This statement in itself was strange as I don't do crazy paranormal stuff.

So everyone was catered for. I walked up the stairs, each footstep felt like a mountain. A mountain I really didn't want to climb and I certainly didn't want to see the view. I went into our bedroom, my heart was racing, I felt lightheaded and sick but no f...er is going to scare me and my family.

I radiated between heightened fear and then anger. I knew what I needed to do. I just needed to be strong. Right, I'm going in! By this I meant going into a state of nothingness. I can best describe it as a vacant mode, it is like you are daydreaming but not fully in the real world. I felt so scared but I am committed now.

I expected to see a huge demonic beast with evil eyes, but what did I see? I saw a dog! Well, I wasn't expecting that. First, I saw a small Cavalier King Charles jumping up and down then I saw a man's hands. I asked to see him but he didn't want me to see his face. He felt gentle and kind but I sensed sadness around him.

I felt humbled that they felt safe enough to show themselves to me and immediately all the fear disappeared. I saw a funnel of light appear, it was time to send them back. I can't articulate what happened but it all seemed so natural at the time. Whatever I did it allowed them to go back to where they should be, home?

I remember his hands so vividly. They were gentle, smooth, creative hands with so much emotion in them. He wasn't happy for me to see his face and didn't want me to see how he had passed but I felt it was all within his hands and his choice.

As a medium, you must always respect the wishes of the spirit person and not push for information to prove survival for entertainment for they will decide what we are to know. I sat on the bed and felt so liberated, humbled, happy and emotional. That poor guy had been stuck in time, it had taken him and his loyal dog who never left him, to do everything in their power to get my attention.

I asked my guides what was all that about and they replied I needed to understand I was capable of so much more and will be doing a lot more in the future but I have to control my fear. It was fear that held me back. No harm will come my way and I must trust!

I learnt so much from that experience, I had travelled all the way abroad to find myself in the one apartment with a trapped soul. If the spirit world wants you to learn and develop skills you really would rather not, you have no choice, you will. I believe there is no such thing as a coincidence and have been proven right, time and time again.

You have so many people in the world hunting for paranormal events for their own gratification. How about some of those so-called mediums and thrill seekers developing their knowledge to help them? There are some amazing people out there who have dedicated their lives to helping trapped souls and returning them home.

These are the true selfless people who often remain anonymous and do such amazing work. (Thank you to all the true lightworkers out there!) I thanked my spirit guides for the honour to work for them but if they could just leave that to the professionals next time, I would be very grateful.

Tony came back from his run and I told him what had just happened and that the apartment would be fine now. The whole apartment felt completely different, I suppose normal. We had no more strange occurrences and the second week of our holiday we were moved to the apartment we were originally allocated.

I was like an excited child wanting to discuss in great detail what had happened but Tony was reluctant. "Jane, I agree it felt like someone was in the apartment. The stools were being moved, it was real, but I can't get my head around it or make scientific sense of it so I don't want to discuss it anymore."

"What, well I do? Are you for real? That was unbelievable! How did that just happen? Nobody would believe us." "Exactly Jane, leave it."

AS ONE CHAPTER CLOSES ANOTHER OPENS

For one reason or another, the church's closed circle came to an end. Disappointing but I felt it had run its course. I decided I needed more experience so I drove several miles out of the area to another church where no one would know who I was. If I did bump into someone I recognised, they would be just as reluctant for others to know what they were doing.

It's strange, although I completely get it. How so many mediums chose to remain private and equally so many want to be known, make money and hit the big time? I've always had this terrible fear of people discovering what I do, to the point it has always been a huge burden to carry and caused unnecessary anxiety.

Anxiety I am completely aware I have created, but struggle to control at times. I love it when I meet a person who completely embraces themself. I'm always fascinated and in awe of them and wish I could be the same.

So off I went to an open circle. This time greeted by two very experienced mediums, one very gentle and loving, the other strict, no nonsense and strangely warm. I spent months there practising on a variety of people, giving readings and doing a variety of exercises these two selfless and committed mediums would teach us.

I loved the fact that each week you would turn up and literally meet such a variety of people, blending with their energy to prove facts that only they knew and work with their loved ones. I also felt compelled to once a month stand up on the church platform and demonstrate mediumship to a sympathetic crowd.

This was laid on for up and coming mediums who wanted to work the churches. Every month, I would absolutely 'cack myself' because I literally hated standing up in front of people but had this pushing force and knowing I needed to do this for the future.

I would always make a good, strong connection and prove through evidence the survival of their loved ones but I just couldn't work out how to believe in myself. People would come up to me and praise my evidence, but still every month I would stand there feeling nauseous, hiding my shaking hands and pretending to be in control.

Once spirit came in and I had the connection, I would feel strong, powerful and a force to be reckoned with. Not only that but to be able to feel the love from the spirit world to the recipient was such an honour, humbling and if I'm truly honest quite addictive.

The only time I one hundred percent felt happy and alive was when I was working for spirit. Nobody in their right mind would stand in front of a crowd, with no preparation and nothing to say and wait for a loved one in spirit to come through, not unless they really believed in what they were doing.

The few minutes before the connection is made are overwhelmingly physically and mentally challenging. As I said earlier once they come in, it is so magical, it completely blows your mind. You ask yourself, how did that just happen? How can I know, see, sense things I don't know?

I've learnt after a long time there is a higher force. I don't know what it is called or pretend to know, some might choose to call it a religious name but trust me, I don't believe in it. I know it is true! This pure, loving divine energy is of such a clever, intelligence far superior to mankind. Not only that but when it chooses, it can heal and produce miracles.

The problem with this divine energy is, if it is

channelled through a medium or healer and they are not from a religious organisation, haven't studied scriptures or have a degree, it is often ridiculed or looked upon with suspicion and fear. I throw a controversial question out there, just perhaps we all have the ability to heal others, merely by the words we speak?

Once again in life it doesn't matter what background you are from, it's the intention of the person that matters. We see good and bad in all walks of life, especially those in positions of authority. On a positive note, there are more good people in the world than bad so don't succumb to fearful thoughts that bring down the energy in the world.

When times become hard, dig deep, look at all you have, even if it's just the clothes you wear. Positivity not only lifts your soul but everyone around you. (Preachy again, too much?)

So every week, I continued perfecting my connection to spirit and once a month shitting myself doing platform mediumship. I remember vividly one Wednesday, there was a large new family who had turned up on the wrong day to see a medium work.

They looked so disappointed that it was only the less experienced mediums working but had travelled quite a long way so decided to see what the night would bring, if anything. Once again, I would sit there waiting to be called to the platform, feeling overwhelmed with fear, hands beginning to shake and constantly needing a wee.

My name was called out and with legs shaking, I walked onto the stage. This is where you start talking to your guides in your head saying, "Don't leave me. Make the connection quick." And although you never doubt them, you start to question yourself. This small window before you connect takes strength, discipline, composure and TRUST.

As soon as I stood up, a male with dark hair in his 60's stepped so close into my energy it felt like he was literally in my body. I began to talk with his character which was strong, rough and straight to the point. I looked at the older lady who was his wife and informed her, her son is abroad and needed help.

I mentioned the name of her grandson which blew the mind of the other family members. I looked down at my arms which suddenly aren't my arms anymore. They have become a thick muscular pair with tattoos on them. I described the tattoos to the family which they immediately confirmed is true.

The spirit is full of character and very funny. I felt myself behaving in his mannerism and saying things I can't remember but made the family laugh. I told the lady I needed to speak to her at the end as he told me very personal information which isn't for the audience's ears but for hers only.

I spoke to the lady at the end and passed on the rest of the message. She was so grateful, emotional and elated. It makes me feel so humbled, what an honour to feel the love from a loved one in spirit to their loved one. The determination of this strong, male character was overwhelming. There was no way he wasn't going to get his information to his wife as he knew it could prevent another loss of life.

That evening blew me away as the connection to spirit was becoming stronger. The only downside was it took my energy as well and I would feel completely fatigued after. This doesn't happen to every medium but I have noticed on my travels a common similarity. Time and time again those who are really gifted seem to suffer ill health.(Not always though)

I have a theory. For some, it's because the spiritual connection is developing too quickly and the physical body can't physiologically keep up. This is when the medium needs to slow down and let the process run its course and not keep pushing the development.

The problem is, it's such an honour, it makes you feel happy, complete and fulfilled that you want to take away any bit of pain for the person who is grieving and make everything better.

Which of course you can't. So those who don't

slow down and keep giving away their energy, eventually become poorly. This is similar to lots of selfless people who continually put others and everyone before themselves.

Shortly after that platform evening, I was approached by Gareth, a gifted medium who I had previously identified as having a very strong connection with spirit but more important a lovely bloke, grounded and normal.

What is normal? Someone I could relate to. Gareth asked me if I would like to join his closed circle. I love the way you find out or fall into new circles especially as I don't believe in coincidences. It felt right so I accepted.

Once again, I would travel even further to another circle. The group consisted of six people all from different professional backgrounds with varying ages. We had a healer, a strong psychic, a paranormal investigator and all round very talented mediums. The characters were all so different but really good, kind people.

I can honestly say this was the first time I felt like I wanted to belong. It was a positive and vibrant group where I was able to show all sides of my personality for it was a safe and accepting circle.

We worked hard and dedicated our time one hundred percent to spirit but always had time for a cuppa and laugh at the end. I never wanted this circle to end as I finally felt like I belonged.

Shortly after this circle, I was contacted by Dorothy who was starting up another closed circle and had invited me. It was such an honour to be invited by such a highly thought of medium there was no way I was going to turn it down.

So during the day I was a full-time mum to three kids, juggling family life and also channel writing for spirit. In the evenings, I attended two circles and participated in open platform practises. I was basically living two lives, one in the material world the other connecting to the spirit world and I loved both equally.

The knowledge and development I was gaining was fast and furious. The channel writing was so natural I could literally just write on demand and what I wrote was at times so clever and emotional, I would find myself frequently in floods of tears.

I thought if these writings make me emotional and I'm ex-military then surely these words could benefit and heal others. The thought had been planted.

Life was hectic but good, I thrived off all the knowledge I was receiving from the spirit world. I have to mention Dorothy's circle was the complete opposite to Gareth's. It consisted of predominantly older ladies and was run in the traditional, disciplined way with dedication and respect.

The whole circle was run by Dorothy's spirit guide which was fascinating. But more importantly, to have the privilege to watch an experienced medium completely trust in spirit and share her gifts was such an honour. There was no room for any egos in this group which was so refreshing. You were taught to remove your material life and just for the allocated time spirit came first.

Each week, the same people dedicated their time which allowed the energy to become easier to work in. One evening, the energy felt incredibly strong and strangely different. I didn't mention anything and just accepted the atmosphere. Whilst we were working, an overbearing powerful sense filled the room.

I found myself bowing and feeling subservient to what had entered our circle. I got a glimpse or should I say they allowed me to take a quick look. There were two dark figures wearing what seemed like hats and so tall they were higher than the ceiling. Now this should be frightening but it was anything but threatening.

It was an honour that these beings had allowed us to witness their presence as if to reward and show us respect for our dedication. This blew my mind, I felt so humbled, grateful and honoured.

The respect these presences deserved was of such importance they could have been of royalty. I can't express the feeling of importance but trust me, I don't bow for anyone and would struggle to bow for any human in the world whatever their status. Yes, I might bow out of politeness but for these visitors I was compelled to.

Once they had left, I turned to Dorothy and said, "Oh my gosh, did you just see that?" Dorothy nodded and we even had a little chat, before returning back to the circle. We felt honoured and I felt emotional to be allowed to witness what I had just seen.

Strangely the rest of the group didn't see what had just happened. Some felt the presence but only Dorothy and myself were given permission to see. Having an enquiring mind, I often wonder what they really would have looked like, as their true identity had been hidden in long black garments.

Perhaps humans aren't ready for that but I know perhaps one day all will be revealed. There are not many things that leave me speechless and I have seen lots of weird and wonderful things that haven't been discovered by humans yet. Or have they?

This experience confirmed that we know so little of what exists and that we must respect all views and not bury our heads in the sand with only the information we have been drip fed. Although knowing or choosing not to expand the mind is less complicated, I'll give you that. Perhaps remain non-judgemental and sit on the fence, at least this won't hurt anyone.

I CATCH UP TO SEE AN OLD FRIEND

There aren't many people who don't use some form of social media but I'm one of them. Every time something exciting or important arises I'm contacted by one of my friends. Even the mums at the school gates let me know if there is anything I should know. Isn't it great, they all spend hours finding out the gossip and I just get the filtered most juicy bits.

I'm contacted by my close friend, Clarissa, who is also a medium and she informed me that my old friend Eddie was travelling down to work in a church not too far from me. I was not a fan of attending church services as it reminded me of my childhood sitting through long, laborious masses. But I wouldn't miss this opportunity for the world.

Eddie is demonstrating. I've never seen him work in public, it's not going to be boring and more importantly, I was desperate to see him. I was so excited to see him for although we have kept in contact through the phone, I haven't seen him in years. The service was just how I had imagined, interesting throughout.

The address, which was a speech about something related to the spiritual reading which takes place first, was beautiful. Unfortunately, a lot of mediums on the speech part usually just talked from their experience which I'm now about to upset some people is pretty dull.

A gifted medium will channel through words from spirit. This takes discipline, courage and also having the capability.

The times I have heard mediums properly channel the address, the words resonate so deeply they touch your heart and soul with tenderness. Also, the lessons and words you receive are deeply thought-provoking and truly beautiful. There aren't many mediums that work this way. Generally they tend to be the older, old-school mediums.

While not all, the majority of mediums nowadays are more interested in receiving and giving messages to the audience. This is important but you can't put a price on a speech directly from spirit, for the words are pure, honest, untainted without any ego or influence from mankind.

Eddie moved onto the second part of the service

which is where the medium makes contact with the spirit world and proves the survival of existence. His information, as expected, was straight to the point, accurate, and kindly relayed. He received a message for someone in the audience who refused to accept the information.

Now, as a medium myself, you know when the message is true and he was spot on. This is where even though you know you are right, you have to make a decision quickly to cut your losses and move onto someone else. Well, I remember Eddie stayed a little too long and repeatedly passed on the words from spirit to this person.

She wasn't having any of it. But you see Eddie would only pass on the truth and if spirit insisted he work, he would listen. This is where Eddie was so committed to working with spirit that he always put them first. Brave, bold and a little funny but not in a strict, stringent church.

I could see the church committee look horrified as he should follow all the procedures and at all times conduct himself and move on. I found this so funny, I had to restrain my giggles from echoing around the building. The joke of it all, was at the end of the service the woman who had repeatedly refused Eddie's messages, apologised and confirmed everything he had said was true.

Eddie was a talented medium but he was too honest. I genuinely don't think he knew how to play the game and be anything other than himself. You would think a church would want honesty as this is what they preach, but even I recognised this wasn't the best place for him.

At the end of the service, a group of people surrounded Eddie to discuss and thank him for his messages. There were quite a few, he had impressed the audience, if not the church committee. Eventually he was on his own. "Hi, Eddie," he looked at me with a distant look as though he knew me but couldn't place where I fitted in.

"It's me, Jane, number 2," that was how I was known as there were two Janes in the first original open circle. He threw his arms around me and held me so tightly. I felt like a vulnerable child who was immediately made to feel protected and safe. "Bloody hell Jane, I thought I knew you but didn't recognise you, as you used to be fatter."

I burst out laughing. He was at times so rude but it really appealed to my sense of humour. It was blissful. We sat and chatted. I got to meet his new partner who was beautiful both inside and out. I noticed he had become a lot older. His hair was completely grey. He had a hearing aid and walking stick and might appear to others as a frail man.

However, as soon as he spoke, he was strong, powerful and more importantly really content and happy. His partner had been the making of him. We talked about old times and I told him I was thinking about writing a book just as he had predicted. He went all quiet and serious and said "Jane, you are going to be famous, don't forget about me." I laughed and said I would never forget about him.

The statement Eddie had made, made me shudder with fear for as much as I knew it was absolutely ridiculous and so far-fetched. I also knew Eddie to be rarely wrong. I made a conscious decision to accept this time he had got it wrong.

I said goodbye to Eddie and his partner, I remember it so vividly. We hugged so tightly and said goodbye and hoped to see one another very soon.

THE GYM, A PLACE OF ESCAPISM

As I've been writing this book, I have been told by my spirit guides that I have to mention my gym story and add it to the book. I have buried this event deep away and now I am sharing it with you. The one place I would escape from the world was the gym, unable to exercise like I used to due to old injuries but a place and time just for me.

Anyway, as time went on, I had this unsettled feeling that only occurred when I saw a certain person in the gym. As you do, I would question my feelings and tell myself to stop being silly. The feelings became stronger and I would find myself doing everything in my power not to be anywhere near this person.

It got to the stage where I couldn't even look at him. I felt a little scared and would start putting a spiritual invisible cloak on myself to hide my spiritual body. Yes I know it sounds weird but that's what I did.

It got to the point where I would be walking on the treadmill, sense his presence entering the room and then spend the remainder of the time focusing on protecting myself and reinforcing how strong, powerful and protected I was.

I hear your thoughts, crazy women! Yes it felt a little crazy, I will agree. So as you know, women like to gossip so I asked a few questions in the changing room and subtly asked if anyone knew about this guy. Within seconds, I was told all the juicy gossip, he was well known.

I don't know what they are called but basically he removed evil spirits from haunted properties that priests and others that had tried before him had failed. He would travel the world eliminating evil energy, spirits and other paranormal activity that couldn't scientifically be explained or understood by man but was very real.

This made perfect sense why I felt uneasy around him. He is surrounded by spirits that remove dark energy so if we look at this situation logically, his team is going to consist of strong, powerful, no nonsense spirits that would have at some time been in dark energy to have the knowledge to eliminate it.

My team consists of light workers, powerful healers, writers and at no time been playing with the dark side. I now knew why at times I would feel nauseous. I even seriously thought about leaving the gym as to be honest I couldn't be arsed with the situation and felt out of my depth.

I was repeatedly told, I was strong and equally as powerful as him and needed to learn this lesson. So as I was just as powerful and mighty as him, I continued to hide as best I could and avoided him at every cost. One thing I need to explain is, our energies were naturally intrigued by each other.

His team would have been drawn to my light on the other side and would naturally venture closer to have a look. I knew this, so I kept my distance and put my trust in my team that were teaching me to deal with the situation and not to feed fear but to face it. I strangely became more empowered and started to believe I was just as strong, protected and in control.

Trust me, every bit of common sense told me to run, but sometimes you have to face your fears, otherwise you can't move forward. The gym had become what felt like a personal battlefield rather than my sanctuary. This went on for a couple of months and I had even convinced myself I was alright and in control.

I was sitting in the jacuzzi having a laugh with one of my friends when, let's call him Michael, sits right next to me. With all that training on how powerful and strong I am, I immediately felt overcome with panic. After a few deep breaths and a strong word with myself and reassurance by my spirit team, I managed to pull myself together.

Strangely, before I knew it, it was just the two of us sitting on the side of the jacuzzi talking to one another. I confessed I was a medium which was completely out of character and then spirit came in strong and we discussed his current situation and revisited his past to help him overcome his future.

Sometimes in life you have to be reminded of who you really are and the foundations you know are true and right for all around. This man led a life of helping others, taking away nightmares and fears we can't comprehend but with this gift he would if not reminded, take a toll on him as a person.

He was and this is no exaggeration like a superhero who literally rescued others and had forgotten who he originally was. To be a superhero, your world is taken over and he was working with such powerful, and yes, to a certain extent, darker energy to help protect others. The right team had chosen him to do good in the world but what a sacrifice to be surrounded in that energy.

I feel the need to explain more about this guy's character. He came across strong, with a very intense stare and as though he had the weight upon his shoulders. After talking to him, he was gentle, soft, kind, loving and strangely beautiful. I would have loved to have wrapped my arms around him and just held him.

His gifts had masked his true identity and so had he. I suppose he had no choice but to embrace his gifts for as I have mentioned before, some people are chosen. Whatever I said that day to him, he needed it, for he was at a crossroads in his life. If I had chosen to run away from the gym, who knows what repercussions would have occurred? The higher intelligence of spirit blows my mind.

That evening, I lay in bed and I felt this almighty blow to the left side of my head. The strength and force was incredibly powerful. It was physically painful and actually made me feel ill. I was suffering with my usual neck and shoulder pain and I'm not kidding, for the first time in years I had no pain, discomfort of any sort anywhere in my body.

I felt young, vibrant and full of energy. It was like a bloody miracle, I lay there thinking, what the hell has just happened. It lasted for roughly five minutes before my aches and pains returned but the power of what had just happened was unearthly. I knew I had been sent healing for I get a mild discomfort in my left temple when I am receiving healing, but this was verging on horrendous.

The force was like I had just been kicked in the head by a horse and that's putting it mildly. The next day, I saw Michael at the gym. I was so intrigued to know everything about him and how he worked but still knew and sensed I needed to keep my distance.

I thanked Michael for his healing as I knew exactly where it came from. He said it wasn't him, I told him, I think you will find it was you. Michael came back ten minutes later and confirmed it was him.

While he hadn't consciously sent it, he told me, I must have needed it. He told me to stop self sabotaging and that it doesn't matter how much I wanted to hide the fact I am a medium, everyone in the future will discover the true me. Great! Something else to look forward to, I thought.

I went home that evening and felt so drawn to his energy for it was so unusual and I wanted to understand more how it worked. I was told by my spirit team our energies are not allowed to mix and under no circumstances are we to become friends. I had done what spirit wanted me to do and that was it, move on.

The more you are told not to play with fire, the more you want to. Every time he would pop into my head, I knew we were instantly connected. It became a discipline of its own, not to allow his energy near mine and vice-versa.

The next day at the gym, I decided I would speak to him and explain we couldn't be near one another. It was dangerous for our energies to be near each other.

I would weaken his energy and there was no room for his team to be anywhere near mine. We basically would weaken each other. I felt sad because I would have liked to have become a friend to him but this was dangerous and I knew it.

I remember vividly stretching on the mat and Michael came straight up to me and informed me we were not allowed to be near each other and I confirmed I had been told the same.

We were both respectful of each other's space and made no further contact. Another lesson I had to learn was to discipline the mind, back to basics and not allow any thoughts associated with Michael to pop into my brain. This was hard for me, as you know, the more you know you shouldn't do something, the more you are intrigued to.

I had perfected this discipline until being told to write about this which has brought it up as though it was yesterday. Fortunately, I also know I have completed this task to open the minds of whoever is reading this book about how amazing life is, also to make you think there are so many people out there carrying such exciting true stories but will probably choose to take their secrets to the grave.

TIME TO TAKE WRITING SERIOUSLY

I was writing away and told by my guides it is time to get a book out. I'm informed it will get published and eventually do well. They also told me it will get noticed within three months. "Really!" I'll have to have a go just to see if any of this is true or I'm finally bonkers.

So not having a clue what I'm doing, as all professional writers do, I decided to check out some publishers by checking the back of the books on the kid's book case.

So, I've got about ten publishers shortlisted and researched a few spiritual book publishers. "This will do," I think half-heartedly. So I completed the book and then I'm supposed to write all these educated things to sell the book to the publishers. Let me make it clear, I'm not a writer so I tuned in and asked spirit to write something.

It's lovely what they have written, but basically told the publisher in poetic words, one way or another, this book is going to get out there. Well, that's going to go down well but what the hell, I have nothing to lose. I sent my book "Mystic Moments in Love and Light" out into the world. I forgot about the book and continued juggling my hectic, tiring but wonderful life.

Over the coming months I received several polite letters from publishers saying that although they found the writings interesting they have basically decided it's not for them. "No surprise there," I thought as I think it's a bit way out there to expect anyone to publish a book written by someone who professes to be a channel writer and medium for the spirit world.

I have to mention *"Mystic Moments in Love and Light Vol 1"* is a book of individual channelled writings consisting of different emotions, healing, death, angel, nature etc. I did find it funny when a spiritual publisher said it was a little too extreme for their audience.

Bloody hell, this book is anything but extreme as it consists of beautiful, gentle, feel good writings. I suppose it was politer than saying "We think your work is shit." Three months later, I received an offer from a publisher and shortly after that, another one. I picked the one my best friend used to live near, why not?

When I told my family, they were all so proud of me. My lovely younger brother, who is a teacher, was really impressed as he knew so many people who have tried to get their work published and failed. "Jane, do you realise how difficult it is to get a publishing deal?" My brother repeatedly stressed to me.

Obviously not, as I was told by spirit it would happen and just thought it would be a good idea to see if it came true. I never had a desire to write a book or even thought I was capable. That was the first time I realised how fortunate I was to be given guidance and help with my work being released.

It had been engineered from the spirit world to reach those who needed it or felt intrigued to read it. I found the whole experience very interesting working with a publisher but the most amusing thing I found was getting the book cover designed.

I had been shown exactly the book cover design I had to get out to the public, basically two hearts, light coming off them resembling the spiritual world and the material world joined becoming one.

The book cover design came back with a variety of different options ranging from scary green misty fog covers to witchy frightening designs. I kept insisting it had to be a light blue background and two love hearts. I never gave up as I had to stay true to the spirit world and eventually the exact book cover I had seen was produced.

I felt such a relief for the writings inside resembled love, healing, nature, not some bloody mystical evil witch producing potions. It's amusing how people can interpret a medium's work.

If you have an open mind and take the time to read channelled writings it really is beautiful and has the ability to draw emotions to the surface you weren't aware you had hidden, very healing.

As the book was getting nearer to being released, I became more and more anxious and fearful. As much as I wanted the book to do well, it would come with a huge sacrifice. The sacrifice of my hidden dirty secret, I am a medium!

I had spent my whole life hiding the true me and would spend years with friends before deciding whether I wished them to know. Hence to this day only a handful of close friends know. I like the fact I blend into society and have no desire to complicate life. Let's face it, life is hard enough as it is.

I continued, still pushing the barriers but now with this dreaded fear of being successful. I'm becoming more tired but reluctant to stop any of the circles as they are both equally enjoyable and I have become really fond of the people in the groups. I remember just before Christmas 2015, I felt so tired and run-down but I had put my name down for another workshop.

Being ex-military you are almost indoctrinated not to show weakness and you certainly don't let other people down. This was a thought-provoking workshop on questioning the philosophy of the spirit world. I was hoping to sit back, expand my mind and just sit in the corner and listen. I had a cold and felt awful and exhausted.

The next thing the teacher said was that they were going to put on some music and we would all have to connect. I thought I really can't be bothered with this and putting on music to connect, what a load of rubbish. Anyway, as disciplined people do, you listen and throw everything into it.

As soon as I heard the music, *Sweet Caroline*, I literally felt a beautiful, kind and loving soul fill my body with her energy. I knew immediately I was with the teacher and it was his wife. She was so easy to work with, it felt like we had become one. I can't remember fully what I said, but the words were flying out of my mouth.

She showed me her husband in his youth, memory links, the jewellery he wore. I felt so energised, on a high of the love from this pure soul to the love of her life. The sensation physiologically running through my veins blew me away. This wasn't just love, this was a love of two souls entwined and connected between two worlds.

This lady was so spiritually gifted it would have been every medium's dream to connect with her. I knew I would have wanted to have been friends with her on the earth plane as she was a selfless, kind, loving woman who always put everyone before herself. I felt honoured that she chose me to work with her.

I felt a little out of it but so high on her love and excitement for her husband. I remember everyone clapping and thinking, bloody hell that was strong and a good connection. For me to reward myself with a pat on the back, trust me it must have been good. Lots of people came up to me at the end and commented on the connection.

Even one of my closest friends, lovely Clarissa, a very well respected medium said well done. It meant a huge amount as she's not the type of person to hand out compliments unless you have earned it. I felt on a high when I got home but shortly after I felt fatigued and lifeless.

The connection was becoming stronger and stronger when I worked, I felt amazing but for some reason I would feel shattered after. Although I put this down to the spirit becoming closer within my body and knew my physical body in time would adapt.

I NEED A BREAK

I decided I'm going to give myself a break. It's almost the school holidays and I'm so tired, I'm really struggling. However, the satisfaction and the privilege of working with spirit if I'm totally honest has become addictive. No more, time to step away. I received a letter through the post from a lady who I met on a course a year or so ago.

I hit it off with this lady, she was fun, vibrant and accepting of everyone, I really liked her. She had hunted down my address to tell me she had recently lost her brother and wanted me to read for her. I wasn't sure as I felt she needed a little longer to heal due to the heartache in this letter being tangible.

I asked spirit what to do and they said I had to, to learn a valuable lesson. What's that then, I wondered? I only ever read for people if I was given permission by my guides and if it would help and hopefully heal them in some capacity, certainly not for anyone's entertainment.

We arranged a date, I got someone to look after the kids and off I set in my car to an unfamiliar area with no idea what I was letting myself in for.

When I arrived, the heartache and pain was everywhere in the air. I still felt it was too early but I was there already. Her partner, I remember vividly, looked at me with disgust as though I am some sort of evil person preying on the vulnerable. To him, I was some sort of smelly piece of dirt on the bottom of his shoe.

The atmosphere felt like they had a heated argument on whether to let the witch in or keep her out of the house. This hurt because I was about to do something kind, allow my body and health to connect to her loved one for no financial gain, just because it felt like the right thing to do.

Anyway I thought, that's the first lesson learnt. I can't reveal what happened in that reading as it's private, but my gosh it was heavy, emotional, heartbreaking but strangely comforting to release some of the worry that her kind, light-hearted and beautiful brother had not felt a thing in his passing and he was safe in the spirit world.

One thing I can mention is throughout the reading, her brother kept insisting she knew something about Margaret to the point where he was not going to let this go. I could feel him laughing and shouting Margaret she'll understand, so I kept pressing it until she said I don't know Margaret but my brother lived in Margaret Street.

I could feel the relief in him for he was trying so hard to prove to her this was real. That day, I pushed and pushed the boundaries to get as much evidence as I could as I desperately wanted to help her start healing. I knew to stop pushing but felt compelled to help. Lesson two, respect the energy you work in and don't force it.

I closed up the reading, spending too long in the energy again, not respecting my energy and thinking solely of the grieving person in front of me. I said goodbye, gave her a hug, took nothing materialistic from the situation but felt I had given my all in helping her. I got home, felt emotionally drained with once again absolutely no energy.

The next day, I asked spirit why they had let me do that reading for it was obvious she needed more time to heal. They said, you were too emotionally involved, you are to be a channel only. What information you received will be the information you need. You forced the process which is wrong and it will make you ill.

It is vital Jane, that you stop forcing your development and start trusting. You need time to respect your physical and spiritual bodies and need time to synchronize and become one. You can choose to listen or make the journey hard but whatever you decide, the same result will occur.

Many mediums have advised me you should always receive something in exchange, otherwise the recipient may not always value you. Unfortunately, we live in a material world where everything, by the majority, is only valued if there is a cost.

Good intended mediums usually struggle with receiving as it feels more natural to give, but I have heard people get really excited about seeing mediums who charge a fortune as they must be really good!

It's ultimately up to the medium but people really need to understand the importance of receiving another's energy that they have entwined with the spirit world. Would you give away your energy/health to help a stranger? Thought-provoking if nothing else!

Just before Christmas, I kept getting phone calls from my youngest child's school asking me to come and collect her. She looked pale, clammy and her heart rate kept racing out of control. I was worried sick because nobody seemed to be able to help me and explain what was going on and why this kept occurring.

As all mothers who are reading this know, our job is to make everything better. I felt so anxious and worried sick for my daughter. It became a regular occurrence. The phone rang and ambulances are regularly called because they can't control her heart rate. I was constantly on tender hooks, "Will nobody help me?"

I prayed to the loving divine, God or whatever it is to help me. I don't care about anything in life, just make my little girl better. Another phone call, I rushed into school. Her little face was so pale and she cried with relief when she saw me.

I told her everything is going to be fine. "I'm here, you are safe now" Deep inside, I secretly have a heavy heart because I can't make everything better.

The ambulance arrived but her heart rate is back to normal. Too late, I sigh. The paramedic insisted we take a recording of her heart, just in case we can find some evidence to why she feels so poorly. I'm not hopeful but kept praying for a miracle. Bingo! They found the suspected reason for my daughter's condition. There is something wrong with her heart.

I'm frightened but relieved we can finally make things better. We went to the hospital where we were referred to a heart consultant. Her condition was diagnosed and they created a plan to treat her condition. They say knowledge dispels fear. I agree but it takes time to process the information.

A very good friend said the most comforting thing that really helped me process the situation and will hopefully help anyone else who might get a health scare in the future. "You are the lucky one, how many people are walking around with conditions they don't know about. Your beautiful daughter will be regularly monitored and kept an eye on."

I can't explain how comforting those words meant to me more than any consultant's advice, for they were wise words and came with so much love. I remind myself daily, how lucky I am.

So I'm sure you will agree, life has been a bit stressful and then I have this stupid nagging fear about releasing my first book, which I know is so insignificant but I can't bear the thought of anyone finding out I'm anything but normal.

My heightened anxiety felt out of control. I'm so tired, run down, looked like poo and I was still trying my best to juggle everything. The book was finally released. I felt proud. Oh my gosh, I am a published author!

I can't really celebrate or share my news as I'm still hiding my dirty secret, I'M A MEDIUM! To be honest, I'm not really interested in the situation as long as my loved ones are safe.

JANUARY 2016 - A MONTH I WILL NEVER FORGET

I walked my two younger children to school, gave them a huge hug, told them I love them and said goodbye. As I walked home, I felt nauseous. My vision felt weird and the ground came straight up fast at me and I felt like I was going to fall.

My balance had gone, I felt dizzy and everything was spinning, I must have appeared drunk as I struggled to walk in a straight line. Thank goodness, I was nearly home because my balance was so bad now, I literally felt like I was on a boat at sea in the middle of a ferocious storm.

That day I rang my husband to pick the kids up from school as I was feeling too poorly. He knew it was serious as I never asked for help as I am a little, okay, very stubborn. The next five months went by, I couldn't drive and only left the house with the supervision of my mum to pick up the kids.

The doctor diagnosed me with labyrinthitis, gave me some medication but nothing helped. I decided to take matters into my own hands and find a cure. I asked spirit if there was anything I could do and they said no, nothing, not until the process is finished. We'll see about that, I'm not getting bloody stuck like this, I thought.

You have probably already gathered but due to my health, I had to walk away from all my circles and spiritual activities, the one thing that made me really happy and complete. I eventually saw an ENT specialist who told me there was nothing wrong with me, he threw my head around in funny positions, which by the way, made everything so much worse.

I couldn't function at all the next day. I was then referred to a physiotherapist who specialises in balance. The physiotherapist agreed my balance was awful and gave me exercises to do on a daily basis. I religiously did the exercises even though they made me feel so sick.

I persevered because I didn't want to be a poorly mum for my children. Surprise, surprise no improvement. I was then referred to a neurologist.

My nightmare was about to get worse. I was diagnosed with vestibular migraines. I thought that's strange as I've never had a migraine in my life but I'm desperate. When you are so vulnerable, you will literally do anything to get better and hang onto any hope.

If this consultant had told me to run around the car park naked and to stick pencils up my nose and in my ears, I wouldn't have seen a problem with that.

I've never got on with medication as I've always been really sensitive to it and one of those people who will try anything other than pharmaceutical products. We tried several medications. Nothing worked, in fact they all made me feel worse and some of you will recognise this with medication, really hungry.

I was then offered a drug for epilepsy which I felt was extreme, but desperate to get my life back, I asked spirit for their advice. I was told under no circumstances I should take this drug and no medication will help me as it is all down to my physical and spiritual bodies being realigned.

I was in a real mess and desperate. I believed this was not a time to listen to spirit for I have a family to think of. I needed to get better and quick. Surely a neurologist knows better than the spirit world?

This proved to be the worst decision of my life, for other people, this would have been a lifeline but not for me. This was the first time I had experienced a full-blown migraine and it was horrific.

I couldn't cope with sound and light. The whole

house had to sit in almost silence. I couldn't watch TV because the flashing lights on the screen were too much for my senses.

I couldn't read a book because it was too much effort for my eyes and brain. I spent hours in bed. I felt ill for so long but thought if I pushed it a little further maybe, just maybe, I will get better. I told my neurologist about all the side effects and he reassured me that for a percentage of people, it did get better.

Military head on, I knew I needed to keep going. I would go out for gentle walks which was such a struggle as it felt I was permanently now on a boat. Fresh air, exercise, pull yourself together Jane, wasn't that what I had told others in the past? I would get home, stretch gently and then weep like a baby on my yoga mat.

I had hit what felt like rock bottom and the guilt of not being a healthy mum for my kids broke my heart. I would have to lay down throughout the day and then pretend when the kids got home that everything was fine. They knew I was ill, because at the weekends I couldn't hide it and they would ask their dad why their mum never came out anymore.

They eventually, as all kids do, got used to mum staying at home and stopped asking me if I wanted to come out with them. I'm ashamed to admit, I went to depths I couldn't envisage. I dreaded waking up in the morning feeling trapped in a body that felt nauseous, off balance with a constant headache.

I felt exhausted from always being upbeat and positive. Secretly, I longed for the darkness, silence, the nothingness and took pleasure and comfort in imagining I was already on the other side. The realisation of the hurt, pain, despair and destruction I would cause made me weep for it was not my time to depart this world.

I had a responsibility and that was to guide my children through this world. I had chosen to have children. Therefore my path had been decided, they would always come first, not my hunger for freedom!

It was when I spoke to the neurologist and admitted I had become very low that he mentioned most people were fine and that he only had to ever section one person due to this drug.

Here I was pushing myself through the side effects when really, I was potentially pushing myself closer to the edge. He also mentioned that nobody really fully understood the brain and they still have so much to discover. Light bulb moment! Time to get off the drugs which by the way takes weeks to wean yourself off.

Another awful experience but worth it in the end. I had numerous brain scans and offered, wait for it, injections in the back of my head. I asked spirit for their help and advice. Please Jane, do not have injections in the head because it will make you worse and will make no difference, they advised me.

So what did I do? One more shot at getting better as my neurologist seemed hopeful. Oh my days! Two injections in the back of my head which was pretty stomach churning but what had I got to lose. That night I lay in bed frightened, my headache was so bad I thought my head was going to explode, no exaggeration.

At one point, I thought I should wake my husband up. I genuinely thought I needed an ambulance but decided to wait and see what would happen. This was one of the most frightening experiences of my life as I actually feared for my life.

Thank goodness the money for medical care had run out as this would stop me from searching for a magical cure. Secretly, I was relieved to no longer feel like a guinea pig being tested on.

I began sitting in the silence meditating, disciplining the mind to a state of nothingness. My connection to spirit became stronger and stronger. I got to the stage where I could walk feeling less wobbly and then spend time everyday sitting in a meditative state before having to lay down. This routine ensured I looked fresh before the kids got home.

I started going out for short periods of time during the weekend. We chose quiet coffee shops with no music and over bright lighting. We would do a recce before sitting down. This was my highlight of the week to finally be able to go out with the kids.

I could finally see improvement. When close friends and family took pity on me, I would tell them confidently I was going to get better.

I knew I was going to get better for I had been told by spirit. Don't get me wrong, I would question them and even get angry for two years had already passed. I had this knowing, everything would get better, but what I didn't appreciate was how long the journey was going to take.

I had at one point been contacted to promote my book but was too ill to do any form of promotion. After a couple of years, I received a letter through the post from the publishers informing me they were terminating my contract as my book hadn't sold enough copies.

Bloody hell, thank gosh nobody knew I was a published author. In my eyes, I was now a failed author with dizzy spells. I really have got so much to offer! So I was pretty fed up and between you and me, I felt a complete failure and had a little cry. I asked spirit what the point was in all of this?

They told me, all I needed was to get my work out there. I needed complete control of my work and they would do the rest. Comforting, but I still felt embarrassed that I had been turned down. Within a few months, I felt stronger and felt compelled to self-publish. I didn't have a clue what to do and felt completely out of my depth.

I sent up a thought asking that the right people at the right time would help me. I began getting my work together and even started writing for short periods, which was a huge improvement and privilege. I could only work for short periods of time because of my heightened sensory sensitivity to light and sound.

Moving objects in everyday life would fatigue me mentally and visually that I would need to lie down for several hours throughout the day to recharge my brain. I eventually improved to the point where I could go for a walk every other day, as this was a sensory overload, especially with cars racing past. My brain and balance would struggle to cope with this.

I'm a stubborn and determined character and there was only one direction I was going and that was getting stronger and better. I would stretch gently, meditate and if I was having a good day, try to write. At 13.00hrs on the dot, I would have to close my eyes and rest to recharge my brain.

The kids would arrive home at 15.00hrs, which meant getting up and being all jolly, happy and pretending there was nothing wrong with me.

Kids aren't stupid, they knew I wasn't well but this routine worked for us as a family. I knew things would get better because my guides reassured me I would make a complete recovery in time.

I used to beat myself up about not being able to take the kids to clubs and the guilt of missing out on the fun things at the weekend would really upset me. Spirit explained to me that children who see those they love struggle in this world will learn compassion, understanding and acceptance of all. Lovely words and comforting but I would plead for them to finish this challenging and bloody awful chapter.

AN INTERESTING TWIST

I had arranged a time to ring a very good friend of mine for a catch-up. I searched for her name and pressed on the contact details. "Hello!" said a familiar male voice that I immediately recognised. It was my old friend Gareth who I had sat in a circle with for a couple of years.

I hadn't spoken to him, I'm ashamed to say, for longer than a year as I had hidden myself away due to my ill health and I didn't want to drain anyone with my health problems. I wouldn't have, but felt so poorly and nauseous with the continuing sensation of being permanently on a boat at sea.

I was still struggling with my daily routine so I had abandoned most of my spiritual friends. It was wonderful to hear how he was getting on and I realised just how much I had missed all my old friends. We had a long chat and I mentioned I felt strongly that I needed to self-publish my work but wasn't very confident as I hadn't got a clue how to go about it.

Gareth immediately told me he had self-published several times and it was easy once you know how to. He offered to teach me the whole process, I couldn't believe it! Not only did I trust Gareth but he understood how I worked. I got off the phone and immediately checked my phone. I must have dialled the wrong phone number and hit Gareth's number.

I checked and double checked the number I had pressed, it had clearly come up with my female friend's name and number. The intelligence of the spirit world is so superior to mankind and to this day never stops to fascinate me. If the spirit world wants you to write or work for them, whether you think you want to or not, you will.

I then rang the friend I was supposed to ring and was so excited I told her what had just happened, but I wasn't convinced she believed me as she, like so many others, needed more proof. But I knew what had just happened.

My health continued to be a problem but I felt like I had a plan. I was determined to self-publish and get spirits' work out there. I felt it could help people. I've been told it will so what the heck, let's give it a go. I must admit, I was also a bit intrigued to see if the future visions I had seen were really going to come true.

What are they? Too silly and far-fetched to share.

So now I continue my daily routine but I have a job and responsibility to the spirit world. Basically, I would write when I felt well enough. Some days, I can write in the spiritual energy for hours, other times, I was too fatigued. Finally, I had found a purpose to get me through this challenging chapter in my life.

I'm meditating, by this I mean sitting in silence with no distraction for longer and longer periods of time. I sensed the spirit around me and learned the art of nothingness. It's beautiful and again an addictive sensation bathing in nothingness. The mind was still, no thoughts rushing around. It really is blissful!

Occasionally, I would feel warmth running through my body, a physical touch and closeness so pure it often reduces me to tears. I was truly grateful for the healing I received but at times, I would beg for the procedure to be quicker. The stronger my connection to spirit, silence, and nothingness, the more I craved it.

Let's face it, my life at that point wasn't exactly thrilling. I often questioned whether this chapter had been given to me to take me away from the world, out of sight and forced to develop my connection. Before this experience, I rushed around wanting to learn everything spiritually like an overexcited child in a sweet shop.

Not only that, but my evidence to prove life exists after death was starting to draw attention. Over time, I noticed with my channelled writing I could write in the energy for extended periods of time. It was as if the meditation was training me to work and connect with spirit stronger and stronger.

The only time I felt full of energy, well and alive was when I was writing with spirit. As soon as I returned to the materialistic world, my health would deteriorate, the constant ache in my left eye would return, including the feeling of sea sickness. I eventually accepted the process as I didn't just believe, I knew I was going to get stronger and in time better. Spirit had shown me the future plan.

I had to get better to fulfil my promise so there was no doubt in my mind, I wouldn't be able to overcome this bloody awful chapter. I felt so lucky and then thought of others who perhaps haven't got loved ones to put before themselves or feel trapped in a repetitive wheel of ill health, or mental disease.

These are the true warriors of society and I am truly in awe of them. I am not going to preach as I can't stand preachy people, but I will give you this. If you can dig deep and visualise being happy, content and healthy, you have to play it over and over again in your mind, feel it, live it, cry tears of gratitude for it. In time it will become yours. I offer no explanation or scientific proof but what have you got to lose?

AN UNEXPECTED VISITOR

Now, as I have explained, I often get unexpected visitors in the night which still occasionally scares the shit out of me, strangely over time you get used to it. To the point where if nothing strange happens for a couple of months, you start to find life a little dull.

I have come such a long way on this journey. I would originally cower under the sheets and plead to God to take all of this away. However, this visitor was so magnificent, I feel compelled to share it.

It was the early hours of the morning and the room was pitch black with a tiny stream of light escaping from a small gap in the bedroom blind coming from the street light outside. I am woken to a sense of calm and serenity. I'm not startled, which occurs frequently, but felt no apprehension, just a beautiful inner calmness.

I looked to the left corner of the room and there was the most breathtaking, naturally beautiful black lady standing tall, elegant and with an awe of authority and power, but gentle. She allowed me to look at her. She was wearing a robe and matching headdress in patterned earthy colours, mostly different shades of brown and reds.

I was fixated on how naturally perfect her face was and how strangely comfortable I felt in her presence. There was a sense of calm and trust. I'm told to turn my head away and lie still, without question I knew this was what I needed to do. As I lay still, I suddenly let out an almighty gasp as I felt a sharp stabbing pain hit me immediately in my right ovary area.

The pain lasted for less than a second but I have never experienced pain so severe. The pain is over before I know it. I turned my head to see the lady and she was gone. I lay in bed thinking, oh my gosh did that really just happen? It blew my mind that this was physical in the material world.

I had been suffering from constant discomfort in my right side ever since the birth of my first child who was delivered by C-section. I had scans but the medical profession couldn't find anything wrong. If you have a persistent pain in your body, it doesn't matter how many professionals tell you there is nothing wrong, we all know our own bodies.

After this lady appeared and gave me healing, I have felt no discomfort in my right side. Let's just say everything is now working as it should! I would find myself replaying the phenomenon, it had to be true as I have never felt such horrific pain and with such precision. My right side had completely healed, no daily discomfort, nothing, all gone!

I'm flabbergasted by this higher, more intelligent, powerful divine energy and start to realise, I will get better, but it doesn't matter how much I plead for the process to be rushed, it will all be synchronised to perfection when the time is right. I'm slowly learning I can't force my life's purpose and have to succumb to the process.

Oh my gosh! I have no control but I'm a control freak! This doesn't come naturally but when you hand over the keys and trust the right doors will be opened, you eventually in time become more content. I have decided when the doors are opened in the future, I will not only go through them but I'm going to leap!

MY HEART IS SADDENED

I was feeling low. It was winter 2017. The weather was damp, cold, wet and very British. I felt this strong sensation and needed to speak to my lovely Eddie. Eddie was constantly on my mind but I felt emotional and weak and didn't want to cry all over him.

The next day, I got a wonderful telephone call from a rough, cockney voice saying, "Alright love, what's going on? You keep popping into my mind," said Eddie. I immediately felt safe and protected. I confessed to Eddie that I was still struggling and finding it very hard to stay positive. I remember his words vividly and they still make me laugh to this day.

Eddie said, "You poor cow, is that still going on?" Only Eddie could come out with such charming words. He didn't sound surprised but reassured me it's coming from my shoulder and neck. I just needed to stay positive for it will get better when the process has finished.

The flaming process again! What am I going to turn into at the end, a bloody butterfly? Eddie confirmed there is also a realignment of spiritual energy taking place. "They have big plans for you Jane, whether you want it or not. It's already happened."

We had such a lovely conversation. We talked about his ill health and how he was waiting to go into hospital for an operation and how happy he was with his beautiful wife. He spoke so fondly of her and you could feel the happiness and contentment in his life. Eddie had, let's say, an interesting life but finally he was truly happy.

He was so proud of his new flat that overlooked the river, one of his dreams was to be able to look out his window and have such a beautiful view. He chatted about the birds he would see out of his window, his happiness was contagious. I felt blissfully happy for him and more importantly he had the most gentle, kind and accepting lady by his side.

I mustn't forget they had a dog named Lily who they both adored. It was a dream that finally came true for Eddie, he had got and finally found love. I spoke to Eddie again before Christmas. In fact we spoke several times which wasn't like us. Usually, we would speak once or twice a year at the most. It felt so good talking but something felt different.

I was woken in the early hours by a huge, dark presence by the side of my bed. I literally sat bolt upright in bed and gasped with fear and shouted out, "Eddie!" As soon as the vision had arrived, it vanished.

I lay in bed, my heart pounding with adrenaline. Had Eddie died? Please, not Eddie! I need him in my life. I couldn't sleep and just lay there in bed, worrying about what felt so real. The joke of it all was, it was Eddie who taught me about these awful premonitions.

The next day, I arranged to meet up with my sister who I told everything to. I don't know but I think Eddie is dead. I wanted to ring Eddie but was too scared to ring him. I pulled myself together and rang him, "Alright love, how are you?" said Eddie.

I sighed such a huge relief. I have never wanted to be so wrong in my entire life. We had another long chat and it was at this point I realised Eddie was more than a friend. He felt more like a father figure. Eddie loved children but for whatever reason had never had children.

He made me feel safe and special, nothing was ever too much and when he had to, he would be firm and direct. I suddenly came over with a strong sense he had been purposefully sent to guide me on this journey. I sent a thought out and whispered, "Please keep him here longer, we all need him."

That was the last conversation I had with Eddie. In January 2019, I received a telephone call from his wife, she said "Jane, there is something I need to tell you." I replied, "I know," Eddie had passed over peacefully to the spirit world.

Eddie had taught me premonitions occur three days, three weeks, three months or three years. Eddie had passed over within three weeks. My heart broke for his wife for they had become one, although my heart was saddened, it wasn't broken.

This disturbed me for I couldn't understand why I wasn't a sobbing mess, especially for someone so special who had literally protected me throughout this whole journey. As the days passed, I just had this sensation, although he had physically died, he really hadn't gone anywhere.

I knew he was still there for me whenever I wanted and as he had assured me at the start of my journey, all I had to do was think of him. I think of Eddie often and tell him to get them on the other side to hurry up with the bloody process.

Occasionally, I feel his presence so strongly, it doesn't make me sad, it makes me laugh as I'm sure he is causing mayhem on the other side. I only have one regret and that is I wasn't well enough to go to his funeral, not for Eddie but out of respect for his wife.

Now I said I would be one hundred percent honest throughout this book so I have to confess writing about Eddie has reduced me to a snotty nosed, ugly-faced crying mess. I've just experienced some sort of therapy!

I think it's because there is no one else I have ever truly trusted and completely let my guard down, especially with spiritual matters. I feel so blessed and honoured to have been guided on my path by a true earth angel. Eddie would roar with laughter at these words and many who he upset would disagree but this was just his disguise. Well, Eddie, you didn't fool me!

A DATE I WILL NEVER FORGET

I continued my life with the same routine every day: gentle walk, stretch, write if I felt well enough, meditation and then a lie down before the kids got home. I constantly reminded myself how far I had come and that I was now able to watch TV as long as the volume was not too loud.

I'm able to go for a coffee, in society! We carefully hunted for the quietest coffee shop. If it was too loud, much to my family's embarrassment, I would explain my sensory problem to the owner and hoped they would be willing to turn the music down. I have to say, most people are really kind and understanding.

Not all though, as some have looked at me as if I'm a freak and refused to turn the volume down, as the crap music which nobody wants to listen to, is for everyone. One coffee chain in particular turns the music down on occasions without being asked. So kind!

It's so thought provoking having a heightened sensory problem as this world isn't really designed for sensory sensitive people. The majority of places you go, especially if you venture to a shopping centre, the music is always blaring out, people are rushing about and the lights are so bright.

You walk outside, the cars are racing by, someone is playing their music really loud, then there is the sound of music from several different shops filtering into the air. Noise simply, for the sake of noise.

Then there is the sense of irritation and aggression, with a mix of sadness, the shouting and whaling of excited youngsters all stirred into the pot. No wonder so many are struggling with the demands of life.

I will never be able to understand how difficult it is for someone struggling with autism or another mental medical condition but I'm strangely thankful to be able to experience a tiny fraction of how demanding society is for them.

I'm ashamed to say, I had never even given others with heightened sensory, any thought, let alone compassion. My heart is saddened to think of so many struggling behind closed doors that aren't well enough to leave their homes.

So many people are unable to go for a coffee because the music is too loud and don't feel confident enough to ask the owner to turn it down, due to fear of being refused and being made to feel insecure and insignificant.

There are so many people struggling in this world and yet we don't give them a thought. We are so wrapped up in each other's rights and what we want, we forget about the silent and often lonely generation.

It makes me feel really angry and passionate that we need to do something, anything to allow those who struggle, feel safe enough to at least have a cupper in a coffee shop. That cupper isn't just a drink, it's a lifeline! It's something you cherish and really look forward to each week.

It makes you feel normal! So to anyone who happens to be reading this bonkers book and owns a coffee shop or chain, turn the music down really low so at least it will stop people from shouting at each other and be able to hear what each other is saying and feeling.

Or god forbid, turn the music off, because the truth is nobody likes it. After going for a coffee in the busy fast world I unfortunately have to go straight to bed to allow my brain to recover from the sensory overload.

This huge achievement reassured me that I'm getting better. More importantly, I'm able to go out with my family and not be left out. This fills me with hope, joy, gratitude and a deep knowing that

I'm getting stronger and better each day.

As I've mentioned before, the time I have spent in meditation is becoming stronger and stronger. What do I mean by this? Well, I've started to notice more frequent occurrences of warmth and feeling a strong presence all around me to the point where it feels like someone is working on my body.

At times, I can physically feel the touch of a person. which remarkably doesn't bother me. I have had several occasions where my eyes start to flicker out of control to the point where I can't physically stop it. The presence feels loving, pure, safe and kind. I feel nothing but safe and relaxed in this energy.

By that stage in my journey, I was so desperate to get better, a unicorn could fly in and heal me and I wouldn't bat an eye. Joking aside, being a medium, you learn pretty quickly what feels right, loving and safe. You have also built up trust with the spirit guides around you, who know exactly who is allowed near your energy.

These episodes become more frequent until eventually it becomes disappointing if nothing happens. I would sit in silence for sometimes up to 2 hours a day, some days fully aware, other times, in what I presume was a deep sleep.

Strange but comforting for why would I receive healing if I wasn't going to get better? I chose to keep this information to myself, except for a couple of extremely open-minded friends.

I promised if I ever wrote this book, I would be one hundred percent honest. This fills me with horror because what I'm about to share, if I can articulate it, many of you will question my sanity.

On the 18th of October 2018, I was sitting in an armchair in the living room about to start meditation or whatever you want to call it. The presence of spirit was so close it was verging on becoming a little unbearable. My eyes started to flicker but this time, each time it would stop, my eyeballs felt like they were being forced back into their sockets.

Then it felt like fingers had been placed up my nostrils and my nose was being lifted up whilst the left side of my jaw was being forced up and out of position. This movement was so aggressive at one point I feared my jaw was going to snap. My head was rotated from side to side with such speed it felt humanly impossible.

The head was repeatedly jolted back and forwards, the chin pushed down to the chest and then the head flicked back again and again. I tried to control the movement but the strength of what was going on was too mighty. I sensed the word trust and thought I'm bloody committed now and wisely chose to relax and go with it.

Finally, the whole body was shaken, the upper body being moved with large strong movements before finishing off with smaller shakes as if trying to get the fluid moved around the body. I was exhausted physically and blown away mentally by what had just happened. How the hell was that possible?

I knew immediately that the headaches were coming from a misaligned jaw, neck and upper left side shoulder girdle. I was also shown pictures of past injuries where I had smashed my head against a hard wooden floor, jumping over a six foot box during my military physical training course and saw images of me whilst weight training dislocating my shoulder which had popped back into position quickly so I hadn't received any treatment.

Finally the penny had dropped why I had been experiencing so many headaches. I had seen every expert under the sun. I had seen osteopaths, chiropractors, acupuncturists but none had been successful. It just didn't make sense; I had continued receiving regular treatments from an excellent chiropractor as she was head and shoulders better than the others.

She had identified my neck and back was causing the problem of the headaches but although they slightly improved they never fully recovered. I didn't breathe a word about this to anyone for months because I needed time to get my head around the situation.

I had regularly worked with spirits and knew they

were powerful and believed in the higher divine, energy, God, whatever you want to call it. However, this was physical, real, tangible, happening in the real world and yes to me!

Every day, I would religiously sit or lie in the silence surrendering myself to the spirit world and trusting the process. At times, I would feel scared as it felt like I was going into the unknown. I needed to get better. I had been shown my future and I couldn't fulfil it if I wasn't physically, mentally, spiritually and emotionally on top of my game.

I had nothing to lose and everything to gain so I chose to trust. On one occasion, I must have fallen into a deep sleep and was woken to the sensation of a spiritual device being put through my mouth to the back of my spine and felt the vertebrae being moved, clicked and repositioned.

The intelligence and precision of the work that was being performed on me was beyond human capability. I started to analyse the process and then decided I had a choice, trust and go with the process or scare the shit out of myself. I quickly came up with the conclusion I was too far committed in this situation to do anything other than get on with it and trust.

I haven't got the words or the ability to describe in detail the continual physiological processes that took place. I can tell you my head was put into end range positions, my neck twisted, turned, cracked and physically manipulated where I felt and heard the vertebrates being moved.

These movements were more precise and different from the normal chiropractor or osteopath treatments; they were accessed from different angles of the body which shouldn't be possible. What do you mean by that? I hear your thoughts.

Well, for example going through the upper clavicle, rib area deep into the body and moving the inside of the scapular, shoulder blade basically and then this would release muscles and relax the tissues around it.

I'm probably not making any sense but hopefully you get the picture, weird and wonderful healing was taking place. The beautiful relaxing, nothingness, meditations had now been replaced by extreme daily physically challenging sessions.

I was blown away by the dedication of the spirit world who were willing and wanted to help me. Why was this, there had to be a bigger picture. I knew and sensed there was an important reason why I needed to make a full recovery. I also was aware I wouldn't be given access to the reason until the time was exactly right.

TIME TO TAKE A STEP FORWARD

After Eddie's death, I had this constant nagging feeling to self-publish my original published work. I was told by spirit, it needs to get out and I have to have complete control and ownership of my work.

There must be no influence over these books for they must remain true. "Yeah whatever, but it would have been nice to have been able to call myself a published author but then who would I have been able to tell?"

I contacted my friend Gareth who told me the process and reassured me how simple it was. The reason it was so straightforward was because Gareth had done all the work and research. He allowed me to use his team of amazing people who, thank goodness, are used to working with spiritual context.

It didn't take long before "Mystic Moments in Love and Light Volume 1" was released and I already had the work written for volume 2 so I set out putting it together. My health was starting to improve and I've noticed I had less dizzy spells but can't seem to shake this woozy feeling as though I am on a boat, which was exhausting.

Imagine using your eyes, balance and sensory systems to steady you upon a ship, some days the waters are calm, others turbulent. Each and every day is different and you haven't got a clue from one moment to the next what is coming your way. This experience has taught me so much gratitude for the simple things in life.

The things I originally concerned myself with are so insignificant. Don't worry about what others think, the truth is nobody really cares and are also probably worrying themselves about what others think about them. You can possess all the material opulence in the world and unless you have your health, you can't enjoy the journey.

For those with good health, don't waste your lives making yourself poorly for material bollocks, otherwise you have become foolish. For those with little wealth, if you have good health and are lucky to have loved ones who care about you, you are the true millionaires.

Not to forget those who are unfortunately struggling with ill health whether that be physical or mental, you are the chosen special few who consist of libraries of wisdom and knowledge. A responsibility to help others, give them tips on how to stay positive and never lose hope.

Hope is a strange thing. For some days it can become and feel a false fantasy but other days it lifts your soul and drags you through each day. How and whatever life throws at you, know this very important fact.

Life can't stay the same, each day changes and so will the hard times. Everything evolves as do you. I was told this from spirit and also folks, please enjoy the boring mundane times for these are precious. They give us time to breathe and catch up before the wheel turns again. Gosh that was preachy again, don't you just hate it when people preach?

So I continued my journey but now have a focus to self-publish. I'm an all or nothing person so I have to constantly remind myself not to push myself too hard and listen to my health which is difficult for an ex-military person who stupidly resorts at times to, no pain, no gain.

This thought process doesn't work and I find myself regressing and having to lie down for longer periods of time. Another lesson I've learnt, listen to what your body is telling you, that's if you want a happy, healthy journey. That doesn't mean wrap yourself up in cotton wool and not push forward otherwise, you won't improve. Be sensible and don't go mad.

A NEW MEMBER OF THE FAMILY

My kids have desperately wanted a dog for basically as soon as they could talk. I love animals but would only own a dog if I could commit one hundred percent.

I am ashamed to admit this, but I must, I was one of those people that liked animals, would stroke them and give them lots of fuss but then be constantly thinking how I could get to a sink as quickly as possible to wash my hands.

Anyway, we had talked about a dog and decided we would go to a registered breeder as we weren't brave enough to take on a rescue dog as we had never owned a dog before. I hear the cries and outrage of so many but that's the truth and that's what we decided.

We looked on the internet at three puppies that were for sale before making the decision to visit and check out the puppies, parents and breeders.

As a family, we had decided on puppy number 3.

I asked spirit which puppy we would get and was told puppy number one. I was a little disappointed but thought it didn't really matter as they were all cute and I would love whatever puppy we were lucky enough to be given. I was supposed to ring up first thing in the morning but for some reason kept putting the inevitable off.

I was a little scared to own a dog because I knew it was going to be a huge commitment and it would be me that would be the main carer. I had mixed emotions flitting between what the hell are you doing, it will be great for the kids and if we don't do it now the kids will be too old.

A part of me wanted to understand why people got so attached to their dogs and loved them so much, surely there had to be something in it? See I have made a pact with the divine, a powerful energy, God, whatever you want to call it, that I will work hard, love this life and every experience as much as I can under the condition, I'm not sent back.

So I have this inquisitive mind that needs to understand more about the power of our furry friends and why we love them so much.

One afternoon, I vividly remember I was supposed to ring in the morning but had kept putting it off. I was feeling nauseous with the decision on whether to make that telephone call. For goodness sake Jane, pull yourself together. It's only a dog, you can do this, I kept repeating to myself.

Finally I rang and asked politely if puppy number three was still available? A lovely, friendly welsh man on the end of the phone said, "Well, that's funny, she was sold until literally a few minutes ago. I only had puppy number one left.

Unfortunately the people who brought her just rang me saying their older dog has got an injury and it wouldn't be fair on the dog trying to recover with a new puppy in the house."

We had a lovely chat about the puppies and their personalities and he assured me I didn't need to rush because he would give me time to talk it over with my husband. I felt suddenly overwhelmed with certainty and said, "I've made my decision. I would like to have puppy number three please."

We arranged a date and I paid the deposit. I got off the phone looking horrified, scared and in shock, what had I just done? My youngest daughter threw her arms around me and repeatedly said thank you as tears rolled down her face. She laughed at me and said she had never seen me look so shocked and horrified.

She was also stunned as she admitted she never ever thought I would actually do it! I immediately rang my husband which I never do as he knows it's only an emergency if I ring him at work. "Jane, what is it? What happened? Is everything alright?" said Tony, worried and concerned.

"I've . . . I've . . . I've just bought a puppy!" I could hear a huge sigh of relief, "Bloody hell Jane. I was really worried," then he broke out in uncontrollable laughter, "What, you've bought a puppy?" How did that happen?

It was February 2019 when our new family member arrived. As soon as I met her I felt an overwhelming urge to love and protect her, she was innocent, vulnerable and very cute. I spent the first week repeating loudly in the house, "I actually like her," sounding shocked that I was bonding with a dog.

The kids kept laughing and reassuring me it was okay and everything was fine. Lottie, that's what we named her, would, at first, have frequent accidents around the house but it was all fine as she was just a puppy. I was blown away by how quickly she became a member of our family and how much joy, happiness and laughter she added to our home.

When friends and family heard we had Lottie they were all a little amused. As I said, I loved animals but I used to think they should be kept outside. Within months I truly understood the connection between humans and animals and just how important they are to our health, physically and mentally.

I'm not a morning person and need to be left

alone to gently start the day. I can force a fake smile out for the kids and the husband but when I see my Lottie, a huge uncontrollable smile and happy positive sounds automatically come out of my mouth. Now that's a miracle as my family will testify!

Lottie without a shadow of a doubt has improved my mental well-being and more importantly has forced me to challenge and improve my balance and proprioception. I would struggle to move my head in different directions as this would unsettle my balance. Looking after Lottie I had to constantly move my head and vision to keep an eye on her.

This was exhausting at first and I would need more frequent rest periods but within months, I could tolerate more head movements which was much better rehab than any professional I had seen. The beauty of owning an animal is that there is someone else more important than yourself, especially if they are very young and this distracts you from your own difficulties.

I have watched and learnt that dogs live in the moment, grateful for a walk in the fresh air, food on the plate and a bit of love. Don't humans complicate life, often never satisfied with what we have and striving for more. We could all learn so much more from our furry friends and who knows perhaps become happier and more content?

THE CALM BEFORE THE STORM

Life is good, I'm accepting my journey and I have finally stopped fighting my health problem. I know it will get better as I was constantly told by spirit and they haven't been wrong so far. So it was time I got on with life and trusted! Amazing things happen when you stop worrying and hand the keys over to the divine energy.

You feel happier, calmer and strangely at peace. Don't get me wrong, it doesn't last long until one of the kids throws in a hand grenade, but once the explosion of whatever life throws at you settles down, you have to keep working at it. I love this thought because it brings me such comfort.

I daily say to the divine, I hand over the keys, you open the doors and I'll walk through them. I now no longer waste time worrying about what the future brings for I know I am protected and the correct doors will be opened for me. I will trust and walk through them. Isn't that great, if you think like this? You no longer need to worry, trust!

It's the end of 2019 and the vibration in the atmosphere felt denser. I was getting a lot more visitors at night which still scares the shit out of me especially when they get right up close to my face. Apparently those on the other side can see lightworkers' energy and are drawn to some of us.

They mean no harm but are just intrigued by our light. Fascinating, really but not much fun in the early hours of the morning. Some get used to it, I'm much more accepting but it still frightens me. I generally see, sense and know. I occasionally hear but send out thoughts asking for this gift, if that's what you want to call it, not to be given to me.

I'm quite happy with the collection of gifts I have and maybe they can give that one, to some other overexcited medium who wants the limelight. Anyway, much to my horror, I have been woken up more regularly by spirit people whispering in my ear. I won't lie, I screamed with fear and woke my poor husband up and then reassured him it was nothing.

One night, I felt a child and then heard clearly the word, "Mummy." I knew who it was but it still annoyingly frightened me. I'm so lucky I have two really good medium friends who are equally gifted in their fields so I always have someone to talk to openly about all of this strange stuff.

I spoke to my lovely friend Clarissa who thought it was wonderful being able to hear and how lucky I was, so I politely said, "Well you have it then!" she also confirmed immediately it was just one of my children in spirit and not to scare them away. I already knew this but it's so nice to have confirmation you aren't completely bonkers.

The other close friend, Becky, is like a professor of spiritual wisdom, a constant thirst of knowledge on how the science of all paranormal and wonderful things happen and why they happen. Not only is she incredibly well read but she is highly thought of and spiritually gifted in her field.

By the way, our conversations are really funny because we have the intellect teaching the unread person who has decided not to read anything, as I want to experience everything for myself without having any other views put into my mind. We have the most wonderful and challenging conversations, where nothing is out of bounds.

She warned me there is a huge shift coming, it will frighten people but it will eventually calm down and this needs to happen to improve the earth's vibrations and hopefully man's behaviour. She confirmed what I was sensing was a shift and energetic change in the world. She then told me I needed to stock up on food as people's behaviour might become erratic.

March 2020, our country goes into lockdown due to the coronavirus. People were panic buying and the shelves were left bare. I had a few bits in but stupidly hadn't taken my friend's advice too seriously. What strange times, home schooling was frankly pretty grim, three kids all with different needs and the eldest, who I fought with on a daily basis just to get out of bed.

Normal family life as I hear from so many. We were the lucky ones as we had a garden, which I would remind the kids how lucky they were just before I could sense a moan coming from their mouths. The world had suddenly been forced to slow down, for many, this was a blessing, for others, their worst nightmare. But it was a period we would all hopefully get through.

This chapter of life apart from homeschooling made very little change to my life, for the life and routine I led before was very similar. I just had more family members to share it with. I must reiterate there were grim times, arguments and hormonal meltdowns thrown in as well.

I can't stand those people who pretend their lives are perfect and mine all of a sudden when I read it back sounded amazing and I suddenly painted myself as Mary Poppins. Sorry folks, I don't know what came over me.

For the next five months I decided there would

be no channel writing unless I was strongly told to. Sometimes you will have no intention of writing but feel compelled to where it doesn't matter where you are, you just need to write things down. I always make sure I have at least a pen and piece of paper with me.

I decided to focus on the kid's home schooling. Once they were settled doing school work I started putting my "Mystic Moments in Love and Light Volume 2" book together. The writings had already been channelled so all I had to do was formulate them into a document for Gareth to process.

The lockdown period was an opportunity to spend time with my children. I thought I knew my children really well but learnt so much more about their personalities, how they thought and got an insight to how they perceived school and the whole institute of society and education.

All three children are so different, they have so much innocence, kindness and love to contribute to this world if allowed to be themselves. I realised in lockdown, I had become one of those mums too focused on my kids doing well at school when although that is great, we all need to make sure institutes of society don't suppress the true child within.

I've always told my children to do their best, but more important be good and kind. I meant these words but had secretly become a parent who wanted my children to pass all their exams, even at the expense of their mental well-being so I could proudly be in the mums with children that academically achieve group.

Well, I decided and learnt I don't want my kids in this group anymore. I want them to be in a well-balanced, happy, kind and loving life group. It's important they remain good, kind and do their best but I don't want them to become sad, low and not enjoy their journey due to striving for bits of paper to please others.

I'm still a nag when it comes to their homework but have this inner beautiful calmness and knowing it really doesn't matter for their futures have already been written. As a parent I can add stress to their lives or allow them to blossom in their own time. Another reality check and learning I received: guide your kids gently but for goodness sake let them be themselves.

I'm a real people watcher and find it really sad especially when you meet a friend and their children are with them, you can see before your very eyes the child has become a mini-me. Their views are their parent's, the mannerisms are the same, STOP! Let the child find out who they are, what they want to be, what goodness and kindness they will discover and contribute to this world. Just a thought!

Homeschooling was coming to an end. I had mixed feelings about my children going back to school.

The kids have become comfortable and we are finally in a good routine. Coronavirus still has a strong presence in society and once they go back to school I'll lose the power to protect them.

Children need to be with their peers to learn how to survive in society, work out what characters are fun, loving and kind and unfortunately what characters are, shall I say, less endearing.

When the kids eventually went back to school, the house was eerily quiet. I decided I was going to have a couple of lazy days, with no routine. Yes that does mean sitting on my bum, watching some daytime trashy TV because I can! I was feeling wild, carefree and naughty but I'm going to bloody enjoy this!

Within two days, I was sitting at my computer frantically writing away but this time the connection felt even stronger. I was able to work for longer periods of time but I'm very aware not to overdo it, as I'm moving forward in life. I still had to rest during the day but I knew there was a finish line in the distance.

Anyone who works with spirit knows their sense of time is different to ours, what they sense as nearly there can feel like eternity to us on earth. I'm hanging onto hope and nobody is going to take that away from me.

I must mention I finally got to see a NHS neurologist who was very pleasant, diagnosed me with a condition that might get better but also might not, there was no guarantee. I was informed I didn't need any of the medication and certainly not injections in my head as this would make me worse, no shit Sherlock!

Another humble pie for me to eat, spirit told me under no circumstances was I to take the treatments offered but I chose to listen to the professionals. I knew, felt, sensed what I was doing was wrong but at the time I was mentally weak, desperate and just wanted to function in the world.

Well, I chose this time to believe in spirit. They told me I was going to get better, so it was no longer up for discussion. I knew I was going to make a full recovery. I had been told, shown glimpses of my future and knew I would have to be better. The only other lesson I would have to learn was patience.

Here's a little moan, if you know someone who repeatedly tells you they are going to get better and is hanging onto hope, whatever you do please don't say to them, "I can't believe you have been poorly for such a long time and you have lost all those years of your life!" These words are meant with perhaps good intention but they really hit hard to the core.

No time in life is wasted, some of us might experience hard times but gosh I have never learnt so much knowledge, wisdom, insight to how others see the world, compassion and humbleness.

Not only that, I have developed and heightened my skills. In fact I will be brazen enough to say, I have grown to like the new me which I would have never discovered if I hadn't been made to slow down and have my eyes properly opened to the world and my old behaviour.

I have in time grown thankful for my experiences, I wouldn't wish them upon another but I'm truly thankful. So, when you hear words of hope, add to them, don't take them away. Preachy bit over!

IT'S TIME FOR A REST, OR SO I THOUGHT

I've been working hard and have completed the book 'Sanity' which consists of positive, uplifting and thought provoking writings for teenagers. I hadn't even thought of writing for teenagers but spirit wants me to, so I went along with it. I've learnt over the years that it doesn't matter what direction I want to work in, I'm always brought back to where they can use my skills best.

I have deviated several times but I've always been brought back to exactly the right place and at the moment they want me to write. I'm really looking forward to some well-earned time off but spirit are insistent. I need to write another book, again for teenagers but this time called 'Clarity.'

It's just before Christmas 2020 and the kids are about to break up from school shortly. This is peculiar, for spirit are not usually in such a rush for me to produce work. I was told, I'm protected and this will not affect my health. The channelled writing will be quick and I'll be amazed at how quick the book will be completed and released. Within three weeks, the book was completed.

The connection with spirit is so natural and easy to work with, but why the rush? I don't understand and I haven't been given any explanation. Finally, I got a rest, the kids are off for the Christmas holidays and I'm going to enjoy it.

Over the break we were informed by the school the kids will not be returning for an extra couple of weeks due to coronavirus, which turned into months. All hands on deck, back to home schooling. I'm not feeling the love for the lack of concern, kindness and well-being for the children but that's unfortunately the society we have created.

More and more school work is piled on top of the kids with not one person asking how the child is coping. My eyes are now opened to the lack of human empathy and sympathy for our future adults.

This I am thankful for, as I learned the importance of having a child that is mentally well-balanced and not just a statistic that exists on a chart to fulfil an education criteria. What about those children who are really struggling? Maybe the parents genuinely can't help them with their maths, or have to work two jobs to juggle the bills.

A lot of goodness has come out of the coronavirus, people showing acts of kindness but also a lot of selfishness, and unfortunately heartbreak and sadness. Children are the future of the world. As adults, we haven't done the best job especially with environmental issues but we could all at least show our kids that people care and that should start in our education system.

Whoops, preachy, just a thought! I feel the rage of some of the readers, for those who have done a good job, this doesn't apply to you.

TIME TO MOVE ON WITH THE TIMES

Now I understand why I had to complete the last book so quickly. I didn't know we would be in lockdown again but the spirit world did, so clever! I've also decided, much to my resistance, that I needed to join a social media platform to promote my work. I knew this was not the way my work will get seen but I needed to stop being such a dinosaur.

I love being a dinosaur! Nobody knew my business and I just blended quietly into society and certainly not drawing any attention to myself. See, I've seen and heard the behaviour of grown adults and parents in the playground talking about social media and how nasty they behave to one another.

I stood by a friend who was horrified another mum had removed her as a friend. They literally stood three metres apart. I told my friend, "Well if you are upset just go and ask her if you have offended her." She genuinely looked horrified at me as if I was stupid. "You can't do that." "Why not? Isn't that what we used to do, speak to each other?"

I don't get the whole social media thing but nobody else was going to promote my work so I suppose I should give it a try. One good thing shortly came out of social media. I was invited into a spiritual group who regularly participated in Zoom workshops on different spiritual disciplines.

I knew it was going to be professionally run as the two people running the group were both experienced, well respected mediums. I'm ashamed to confess I have never been on a Zoom call so I know it will push this old dinosaur out of her comfort zone.

So on the first spiritual Zoom call, I decided I was going to sit quietly and listen as I was very reluctant to press any of the frightening buttons. The course was going really well and very interesting. I was having a nice time. Something was said and I felt an urge to start writing. Oh no! I don't want to speak on Zoom!

My throat was constricting and I knew I had to read what I had been given. I also know exactly who was going to reply to the comment as I had been shown. So the lovely instructor said, "Has anybody got anything else they would like to mention to the group?" Here goes, I put up my hand and hope I'm going to press the right button.

Much to my astonishment, this Zoom thing actually works how it's supposed to. I told them I had something from spirit, which was very well worded and quite profound. Not my words! Immediately, the lady who I had been told would reply, started to preach to me as though they were my words.

I remember feeling nervous and replying to her suggestions and then I suddenly felt spirit come in, but this time it was so strong. I felt confident, powerful and as though I had real authority. I knew I was speaking words of wisdom but couldn't remember what I was saying until the end where I became fully me again.

I put some friendly nice words at the end to please the lady hoping what I had said before hadn't upset her. I spoke to a very close friend who was also on the Zoom call and asked her if what I had said was okay. She assured me I had spoken with authority, straight to the point and there was no argument or disagreement to what had been spoken.

That was the first time in years I had spoken in public with spirit and I have to admit, I was shocked by the strength, improvement and extreme closeness of our connection. I had been told I would feel strong and confident when I worked in the future but until you experience what they are telling you, you still question them.

Each month, this group would put on different workshops and the next one was a regression course, something to be honest that doesn't really interest me. I think life is complicated enough without dragging up past lives. I tell myself it's good to be open-minded and if nothing else, I'll get to practise on Zoom again.

What I hadn't realised or put two and two together was I had been sitting for the past five years in long periods of silence perfecting my ability to go into a deep trance state in a very short period of time. Anyway, the day came and I was more curious to play with the Zoom buttons to see if they will work again.

Two lovely ladies were running the session. They got us to do a couple of breathing and relaxation techniques followed by some guided meditations. I was really enjoying the exercises and feeling really excited to be in a group of people and working with others. I found all the guided meditations natural and felt a sense of ease.

"Right, everyone, we are going to do a proper regression. It will just give you a taster, we won't be going too deep," said one of the teachers. "Sounds good, it should be interesting," I thought. I'm sitting in my study at home feeling relaxed and ready to fully commit to the process.

When I'm working with spirit, I'm one hundred

percent committed and as I mentioned earlier, I hadn't fully appreciated how quick and easy it is for me to go deep into a trance state. We are guided through deep breathing and relaxation techniques and I can already feel myself going into a trance state.

We were told to step into an elevator and we are going down, counting backwards from 10 seconds. The lift stopped and I was guided through the voice of the teacher to step out and walk down a misty red corridor. I remember thinking I don't like going down and not keen on this misty red, it was a bit creepy!

My guides sensed my scepticism and I could feel them surrounding me. I felt both my hands being held which brought me such comfort, I felt like an innocent child. I now know I have to completely trust, for I need to experience whatever is in front of me, there is no room for fear.

When you can physically feel your hands being touched, all fear is immediately eliminated as there is no doubt, you are protected and loved. So I continued down the corridor but it feels like the walls are narrowing and I feel a little nauseous. We stepped into another lift and once again we're going down, down another corridor.

This time, the floor was covered in a red carpet leading to another door. We went through the first door and then saw a second door which was blue. I stepped through the door into bright daylight and onto a busy cobbled street full of hustle and bustle, with the chitter chatter of excited people.

It all felt familiar as though I frequented this place often. The ladies were dressed in long ankle length garments, nipped in at the waist and wearing bonnets. The gentlemen were wearing long dark tailed coats and tilting their top hats in recognition.

I noticed the old fashioned, beautifully maintained shops, the wooden varnished surroundings of the windows and doors that have been polished to perfection, with love and pride.

I felt totally at ease, content and happy, I suddenly felt compelled to look down. My shoes were well cared for, they had white material on the top with brown buttons and toe caps. I was a woman in the 1830s wearing a bonnet and a frilly blouse. I had a tiny waist and a long slightly puffy skirt which was down to my ankles.

I was so happy, vibrant and carefree, not a worry in the world, smiling pleasantly at the people passing by and life was good. I'm looking around and I want to explore the surroundings. I see the birds flying by in the clear, blue sky. I can feel the breeze upon my face, a faint smell of smoke lingering in the air and the smell of the horses pulling carts trotting past.

There is not a doubt in my mind, this is who I am!

As I walk further down the cobbled street, I notice very poor, dirty children wearing torn clothing and their feet are bare. I have a woven basket which is full of bread and apples and I start to hand out the food.

The children know me as I know them, as if this is a frequent occurrence. My heart fills with joy to see the gratitude on such young unwashed faces and I feel hope, love and a strong protective desire to help them.

As I walk a little further down the cobbled street, I feel the presence of a tall threatening man with rotten teeth approaching me. He is so close I can smell his vile dirty, stale, smelly odour. I shudder with fear and my stomach churns with anxiety as I'm now standing in a narrow side street with no one else around and it's eerily quiet.

I hear his deep rough voice which tells me with a bullying and aggressive tone not to feed the children. Otherwise they will not work. The man steps forward, pulls a sharp object out of his pocket and stabs me in the left side of my chest and then the right side of my stomach and then continues like a crazed wild beast slicing repeatedly up and down my back.

I'm lying in a pool of blood lifeless with my legs hanging out and strangely, I'm looking at my shoes. I realise I'm no longer in the body of this lady but watching from the side, out of the body.

Before I die I hear myself clearly, in a distressed voice say, "But who will feed the children?"

I suddenly hear the voice of the lady taking the session tell us it's time to come back. I'm speechless, why the hell have I just experienced this? It was not only terrifying but really upsetting. As a group, we were then asked to share our past regressions. I told the truth but kept it short and straight to the point.

I needed time to process what the hell had just happened and didn't want to cry in front of anyone, let alone on a Zoom call. You'll be happy to know everyone else had happy, wonderful past regressions, a couple struggled and I think a few might have fallen asleep but it was overall a very positive experience for the majority of the group.

I wanted to understand why I needed to witness the past because I can assure you, if I had full control over the past regression, I would have made up something a lot more uplifting. I asked spirit why and was told I needed to understand why I have this inner deep seated fear which has been with me since I was a child.

As a child, I would cover up my heightened fear to every experience in life, everything in my life, school, sports competitions, speaking aloud, the military which I have to mention taught me very quickly how to hide any signs of weakness. But as much as I might appear confident to the world, my inner fear always felt extreme and out of control.

I also have to mention seeing dead people as a child probably contributed the most! I decided to document the past regression. I sat down at my computer with a heavy and anxious heart as I didn't want to revisit the experience but had a strong desire to explore the past.

I wrote down step by step what had taken place even that awful narrow red corridor that had previously made me feel sick. The emotions poured from me, tears, hurt, fear and anguish all flooding out of me. I have experienced a lot in my life but I have never felt heartache that physically shuddered through my veins.

It amused me how something that had happened all those years ago still had such a tight grip on my behaviour today. I wrote down every detail, made myself face that evil man, looked him in the eyes and knew I had to allow the process to be completed, not missing any detail of the event.

It was truly awful, frightening and traumatic. I wept like a baby, out of control, my chest hurting from all the crying and deep breathing. After revisiting this past regression, I genuinely felt calmer and at peace with myself.

My husband even mentioned how I had become more content and relaxed and trust me, husbands are a good gauge on change as blokes aren't always the most aware of what's going on in a woman's head.

It made me question this whole past regression life thing. I have always sat on the fence with this topic as I just think keep life simple. I'm thankful for that workshop, although it was challenging, there had been a significant shift in my fear levels. I feel happier, more content and a little more in control.

Fascinating past regressions that's if you choose to believe. Imagine we could all be walking around with tiny fragments of past lives attached to our energy that we haven't dealt with. I can't prove any of this is true but I do know what I experienced and I'm finally free of that overpowering fear I have carried since birth.

TIME TO WORK

I was starting to feel stronger. I can do more throughout the day just as long as I avoid sensory situations, bright lights and noisy places. I have worked out this formula and if I stick to it, I've got a really good quality of life. I tried to give up my rest time during the day but my brain can't cope with it.

I was thankful for the breakthrough in my health, but frustrated. This was another sign of improvement for the real Jane was getting more feisty and eager to get fully back in the game. The next spiritual workshop is a chance for mediums to work for others, giving proof of the survival of those who have passed over.

I knew with the two mediums running the workshop only the best evidence would do and that's exactly how it should be. None of this 'airy fairy' evidence, talking in spiritual symbols, proper facts, memory links, how the person died, the relationship of the person, names and most important, something that will give the recipient no doubt in their mind who their loved one is.

I felt this urge to ask if I could work as nobody was going to volunteer me as I was still very new to the group. The majority of the mediums in this group have been working the churches for years, incredibly experienced and how do I put this politely, of the more golden years.

So I hum and haw about it and decided, what the hell this is probably the safest place to work and the ladies are really kind and supportive. I contacted the organisers who decided if it is okay for me to work. As I was a member, it was agreed I could work, every detail was run by the book.

The day finally came. I was feeling anxious but decided to trust spirit. If they didn't want me to work, they would have engineered it so I couldn't have. It started off very gently and I was put in a room with a gentleman of Nepalese descent who spoke broken English, so I knew I needed to be precise and accurate.

I immediately make a strong connection but the recipient can't identify them, so I try again, still no understanding. I move that person to the side and pick up a little old lady who I think would have no connection to him. I continue to explain the room, it looks like a care home and I describe the waterfall picture on the wall.

The lady keeps repeating "my boy." She was so thankful for his kindness and care towards her and that he made her feel special and loved. The excitement and gratitude of this lady being able to pass a message on to him was beautiful. As I have already explained before, as a medium, you get to feel the emotions and love from one world to another and it's a real honour.

The gentleman in front of me didn't say very much which can be a little nerve racking as you can start to doubt yourself. All the working mediums were called back to the main screen and the recipients were asked how their medium had performed.

My gentleman with a straight face and very little expression, explained he used to work in an old people's home and was thinking about this lady I had described and she was the only person who had ever called him "my boy."

They had a very close relationship and she had allowed herself to trust him which was very hard for her as she was of a generation where she didn't want a male carer. I could see through pictures in my mind how caring he had been towards her and always ensured she kept her dignity in delicate, personal times.

He also went on to say he remembered the waterfall picture which I had described in detail. The only criticism I received was I only needed three pieces of evidence and gave too much. I have to admit as soon as I felt spirit draw in, I felt alive, happy and complete, and yes a little overexcited for it had been a few years since I had done a reading for someone.

When you work as a medium to relay messages, the energy is really heightened. There is so much going on, feeling the emotions, talking and communicating with the deceased one. I tend to want as much information as possible—smells, feelings, memories but most important I search as a detective for the emotional link that will blow the mind of the recipient.

It's so rewarding working for spirit but it has its drawbacks, as well as loving memories you can find and see things that aren't always positive. A friend or family member might desperately want to say sorry for something horrific they did towards this person on earth.

I'm not going to flower this up, at the beginning it did upset me but you have to learn you can't carry other people's journeys on your shoulders. Otherwise you will make yourself ill. A person who offers counselling has a system where they can talk through the trauma they hear.

A medium has no one, what goes on in that sitting should stay confidential. A counsellor will have time to get to know the client and perhaps have an inclination of what is coming. A medium has no clue what will occur until the event. I do suspect this might have an effect on most mediums' health. You have to learn quickly to deal with it or walk away.

Another reason perhaps, so many mediums tend to be older as they have more maturity. On a positive note, a good medium will get straight to the issue of a client, which will only be received if the spirit world knows the person is ready to process, again far superior intelligence than man can obtain through study.

I was pleased with how the first reading went and thankful that spirit came in so quickly. Sometimes you doubt and have a little wobble before you do a reading because it's not like you can prepare or take notes before, it's all on trust. The next thing the mediums are asked to do, is a demonstration to the whole group that's if we are happy to.

I'm asked if I'm confident to do this. The truth is I want to shout, "NO!" but I find myself agreeing to the challenge. Guess what, I'm only bloody asked to demonstrate first! I feel panic, anxiety and horror. Then before I know it, I'm talking away giving information and proving survival after death which seems like a hundred miles an hour.

The strength and love of the person coming through is extreme. It feels like I have become the person and she is so close within my energy, she feels like she is inside of me. I know immediately who the message is for and the lady who is working with me even starts to boss the recipient around.

This beautiful, kind lady from the other side is on a mission to get out as much information as she can and the love she passes through is truly breathtaking. I'm on such a high at the end. I don't really know what has happened. I remember everyone clapping but that's it.

I'm sitting on my chair and I can feel lots of people surrounding me desperately waiting for me to relay their messages. All the mediums have the chance to demonstrate and every time the leader asks if anyone has a message, I'm putting my hand up and relaying messages, the strength and power of the connections is off the spectrum.

I'm feeling highly wired, full of vitality and energy as the spirits of the loved ones become increasingly closer. At the end of the workshop, I felt exhausted, delighted the connections had gone so well but a bit freaked out by how the spirits used my body to communicate and how naturally it occurred.

The last five years, I felt frustrated that I couldn't participate in developmental spiritual groups, but the training of sitting by myself has proven to be more beneficial. It did cross my mind whether the spirit world wanted me to be hidden away to develop in their pure energy. The results were good and I was once again excited about my future.

The next two days, once I had come down from my

high, I crashed with exhaustion. The headaches became worse and my balance had regressed but I thought it was worth it, as at least I knew I could still connect to spirit for others.

My friend Clarissa, who was in the workshop and had seen everything on Zoom, rang me up. "Oh my gosh, Jane, you were on fire! What are you going to do with your mediumship?" I sadly told her, nothing, as I had been sick, my energy is just not right yet.

She comforted me and said, "Well, at least you know you can still do it and when the time is right, you will." Clarissa has been there since the early days when I first stepped into a spiritualist church, we have laughed and cried with one another. She has kept me strong and focused on the bigger picture working for spirit and I am eternally grateful.

I needed to understand why I had been given such an amazing gift if I can't use it to help others. The answer was direct and straight to the point, all we want you to do for us is write. Nothing more, nothing less, we need your dedication and commitment to write.

You have been shown your future and the only way you can go onto help others is write, we will do the rest. Okay whatever, I'll write. It was like I was an unruly child who had to be shown I could still work as a medium for others before accepting the role spirit wanted me to do.

Working as a channel writer for spirit doesn't take any of my energy. I feel ignited, healthy and fulfilled. Maybe this has been engineered by them as I know, that if I was able to do both I would.

The excited child would combust and it was for my benefit I needed to concentrate on what the spirit world wanted me to do rather than what I wanted to do. I sometimes laugh why I have been picked to write for the spirit world as I'm not exactly conforming and compliant.

I DIDN'T SEE THIS ONE COMING

The children are back at school and it felt like some sort of normality was returning. Yes, I'm still getting spiritual visitors in the night and have even started to become almost disappointed if nothing unusual occurs.

It's taken such a long time to feel happy within my own skin, some people in a lifetime never discover or accept who they are so I'm really grateful. Although don't get me wrong, I'm not going to announce to the world I'm a medium.

I'm happy with life and even okay with my health. I'm still receiving daily healing from the spirit world which is thankfully less aggressive with my neck and jaw, but nevertheless it's still occurring.

When I first received this physical healing, it terrified me for let's be honest it is not exactly normal! I would have to reassure myself I was safe, concentrate and try with all my might to relax and trust.

Now I really don't bat an eyelid, it's actually become part of my daily routine. I know I am safe, in loving hands and it's also the only way I am going to get better. It's a wonderful feeling when you stop fighting and pushing forward things that you really can't control.

What is it we are all rushing to, I often wonder, the grave? I have this inner feeling, knowing, I don't know how to articulate it, but everything is going to work out exactly fine. Something has changed within me and I really like it.

I'm starting to write random notes in my exercise book, dates of events from the past. I have a suspicion but they know I'm not ready to do that. Anything but that, I think. I'm pottering around the house and I'm told quite clearly it's time for me to start writing again and it will amuse me.

I had my suspicions where it was going but I didn't want to connect properly to find out. Maybe I'll leave it for a few days. I was waking up in the night having to write down past events, I needed to document everything. It was a Saturday and I've just finished a Shamanic workshop which was fascinating and really opened my mind to how nature, animals and the spirit world can work in harmony.

I'm a great believer in learning as much knowledge on all beliefs and philosophies as possible and how important it is to respect each other's views. That doesn't mean I choose to belong to any, but I have a respect for others' beliefs, even if I don't always agree.

Being brought up as a Catholic, I had very little knowledge of any other beliefs or philosophy and still to this day can't get my head around how and still they cause so many wars. If I was in a position of mighty power, I would create one way of life.

The rules would be, love everyone and everything like there is no tomorrow. Treat earth and nature with respect and it will provide shelter, food and protection for you. Learn from animals how to take a day at a time and be grateful for the simple pleasures of life.

Don't judge people for being different, embrace them for they bring interest and colour to the world. Last one, for goodness sake just be kind to one another. Unfortunately or fortunately, I'm not in a position of power but I think the above could eliminate a lot of unnecessary problems. Preachy!

After each spiritual workshop I attended, the best bit is the telephone call with my close friend Clarissa. We discuss what we think, the bits that worked for us and more importantly, if we would use any of it in the future to progress and enhance our medium skills.

I love these chats because we are completely honest because we have known each other for so many years, sat in the same circles and know it is safe to be completely open. It always makes me laugh when we catch up, it doesn't matter how hard the other tries to hide what's going on in their life, the other always immediately knows and asks the correct questions.

"You are writing another book soon, what do you think it's about?" Before I have time to answer. "They are going to ask you to write about your journey, that will be a challenge for you because you are so private." said Clarissa.

I confirmed I have my suspicions, but I have decided to put off asking them as I was not sure I wanted to hear the answer. Clarissa then throws in another comment, "I've just had a funny thought, they might make a film about it." We started laughing as we both knew this would be my worst nightmare as I'm not interested in anyone knowing my business.

We decided what will be, will be! We knew how the spirit world works and if that's the bigger plan, no amount of fighting against it will matter. Even as we talked about it, we both burst out laughing as we knew how ridiculous our conversations would sound to anyone else listening.

The next couple of days, I was having random flashbacks of things that have happened in the past, sad personnel events, strange occurrences and people who had helped me. I had a strong compulsion to write all these images and thoughts down. "You need to write again, Jane, it's time, you will find it amusing."

I knew exactly what they wanted me to do but when I needed clarity, truth and confirmation, I would always sit down at my computer and tune in to make sure what I'm receiving is one hundred percent accurate. I'm not about to do something I really don't want to, unless it is absolutely necessary.

As soon as I started typing there was the usual constriction of the throat which was immediately present and very strong. This, I must explain, is how spirit choose to work with me as with many other ways.

Spirit predominantly uses my throat to work with me and through me. It's comforting especially when you are in need or send thoughts for help as you can physically feel them near you.

It's taken many years of battle, fear and acceptance but I have grown to love this sensation for I'm immediately made to feel protected and in safe hands. It's also handy when you are in the presence of a dangerous situation or near a lower energy, perhaps a volatile person. You can plan to make your exit and remove yourself subtly from the situation.

It's so funny listening to myself talk as if this is perfectly normal, trust me, at first, I thought I had something medically wrong with my throat and didn't like it at all. Basically I'm told, surprise, surprise! I have to write about my journey.

Writing about my journey would catch the imagination of the readers more than my previous books but eventually, perhaps intrigue the reader to read the writings from spirit.

I could see how this might work as I channelled the other books, I used to wonder how and why people would even decide to read them. I'm not deluded, there aren't many people who would rush out and buy a book of channelled writings from a so-called medium.

I thought perhaps you might get a handful of spiritual people but really they need to get to everyone. So I said in my thoughts, that's great but you know I'm a private person and just coming to terms with the fact it's okay to be a medium.

I had always thought one day I would write my story but when I was in my late seventies, perhaps even admit it was me. Still hadn't quite decided, kick the bucket and watch the mayhem with a cupper on the other side. Now that would be a great inheritance to leave the kids!

Working with spirit as I've said several times doesn't always go the way you think it will. You have thoughts sent your way but they have already engineered the process, so clever. I'm uncomfortable with this decision but I also know it's the right thing to do.

It will help others and if they are drawn to read the other books their hearts and souls will be, perhaps gently healed. Right decision made, I'll do it! I comfort myself that I have nothing to worry about unless it's ridiculously successful, but even then I can always hide away, surely?

WRITING A REAL BOOK

I find the task of writing a book that I actually have to contribute to a huge ordeal. As a channel writer I literally sit in a beautiful, pure energy and then the magic begins. My spirit team draws close and I just write. It's easy, I don't think, I just write. The writings I receive are beautiful and I would love to be able to say they were mine but I'm just the secretary.

I had a little chat with my spirit team asking that I'm going to need their help and they will have to work with me on this one as they already know my English is mediocre. I mean really, they could have picked anyone! So I start writing and the interesting thing is, much to my horror I actually have to write by myself but they are steering the journey.

I don't have to think about what I'm going to write about, I'm taken there. I decided throughout writing this book I didn't want to write about the gym scenario and the near death experiences but I was made to go back. The other thing you might have noticed reading this book, I'm limited on the words I use as I don't feel a desire to use words that not everyone can understand.

Occasionally a new word will pop in which I have genuinely not thought of, simple but different for the reader. The first few weeks of writing I would waver through feelings of panic that I can't do this, feel overwhelmed by feeling inferior to those proper, educated people who actually understand written grammar.

As I progressed, I became strangely liberated and started to enjoy it. Throughout writing my journey I have been made to look at previous events. This is something I don't often do as I'm a person who tries to enjoy the moment and I think it is important not to dwell in the past.

I've learnt sometimes you have to go back to be able to go forwards, although I still believe you shouldn't stay too long in the past for we all have so much to add to the future.

I've also learnt I hadn't processed some of my experiences and found myself on several occasions in floods of tears and doing that really ugly face crying thing which was rather and strangely calming.

So what is next, well this is the part when I desperately wanted to tell you I had made a complete recovery from my health hiccup, as I have been told continuously but I'm still waiting for the final piece of the jigsaw.

I had already dedicated in my mind a full chapter to how spectacular it was going to be and how I fell to the floor with tears streaming down my face, yelling the words, thank you, thank you! I'm still waiting for the final completion of my health but each day I am becoming stronger, happy, alive and ready for the next challenge that is coming my way.

I know I will be fully recovered, I have to be, for what I have seen, it would be cruel not to be. Life is wonderful, exciting, unpredictable and at times cruel and bloody hard. I have to mention one really important thing I have been taught. When life is fantastic, happy and wonderful, just enjoy the moment.

Don't allow others or yourself to weaken the sensations you are experiencing, bathe in it. When times are mundane don't complain, enjoy! For you are being given time to breathe and think. When times are hard, sad and appear dark, know in your heart that nothing in this life stays the same and it has to move on.

Your hurt and pain will feel unbearable, but it will, day by day become better. For those who have perhaps lost a loved one, a fragmentation of them will remain in your heart forever and if you choose, cannot be parted.

We are here on earth for such a short period of time in the big scheme of things that it's not only exhausting but a waste of time worrying about what others think, say and do.

With a passion, belief and deeper knowing you can and will achieve whatever it is you want from this life. Start really believing in yourself, see the beauty and fun in everything. Laughter and fun is so powerful it lifts the souls of not only the people directly involved but all around. Be aware whether you choose to believe it or not, like attracts like.

This journey is full of enough happiness for everyone, it's just your choice to grab it. I hear your thoughts, how does she know she's been ill the last five years, so she is obviously doing something wrong. Correct!

I have, the main one not allowing myself to accept who and what I am. I've also learnt a wealth of knowledge on the way and if perhaps I had of just listened to all the words of advice I was lucky enough to have been given, I could have had an easy life. But you know what? I can't think of one thing I would want to change.

A FINAL FAREWELL

So I have finally finished the book, what happens now? I will send it out into the big wide world and put it in the hands of spirit. I have been told all along, all I have to do is write, they will do the rest. I shall sit back and wait to see what happens.

Is this all a lot of nonsense or has it all been true? I struggle to believe this book will be successful but have a knowing deep inside this to be true. I have decided not to think or worry about the future and have decided to hand my keys to open the next door to spirit.

I was born a medium and that is who I am. I no longer apologise for seeing dead people and bringing comfort in the words I write and speak. Society and beliefs are put upon our young at such a fragile age. Maybe, just maybe, some of us are supposed to be born different, maybe that's a higher loving divine plan for this world.

Maybe man has become too blinkered by indoctrinated views? Just maybe one day this world will embrace everyone and everything how it's truly intended. Whatever you are, or choose to be, if you have a loving heart and want to bring goodness into this world, go for it!

I have seen my future and I'm not best pleased with what I have been asked to do next, but sometimes in life you have to be brave and own what you represent. I have made a conscious decision with my spirit team that when all of this, far-fetched, insane, crazy and bonkers next chapter occurs, I will rise to the challenge.

I will in the future be laughed at, ridiculed and unfortunately thought to be something evil but I also know this will come from the fragile, scared and hurt inner child. I will also receive uplifting, kind and loving words. This book will enable others to talk about their unconventional experiences perhaps they have hidden away.

One thing I know it will do and that is, make everyone question whatever beliefs if any, there is something very real other than us and it is superior, more intelligent, kinder, more loving, accepting of all and literally just a thought away.

When this prediction comes true not only have I written about it but I will have proven this is true. Scientists will say the usual, there isn't enough evidence. I reply no, you just haven't worked it out yet.

Then we will hear it's a coincidence, as much as we can debate the topic, when you work with spirit you quickly learn there is no such thing.

I hope you have enjoyed my journey and if nothing else it's made you laugh and expand your mind. Remember life is wonderful and what you make it, who knows, the reluctant medium could be out to play very soon!

The End

Printed in Great Britain
by Amazon